The Effectiveness of the Sarbanes-Oxley Act of 2002 in Preventing and Detecting Fraud in Financial Statements

by

Debra L. De Vay

ISBN: 1-58112- 318-3

DISSERTATION.COM

Boca Raton, Florida
USA • 2006

The Effectiveness of the Sarbanes-Oxley Act of 2002 in Preventing and Detecting Fraud in Financial Statements

Copyright © 2006 Debra L. De Vay

Dissertation.com
Boca Raton, Florida
USA • 2006

ISBN: 1-58112- 318-3

THE EFFECTIVENESS OF THE SARBANES-OXLEY ACT OF 2002 IN

PREVENTING AND DETECTING FRAUD IN FINANCIAL STATEMENTS

A Dissertation

Presented to the
Faculty of the Argosy University–Orange County

In Partial Fulfillment of
The Requirements for the Degree of

Doctor of Business Administration

by

Debra L. De Vay

January 2006

Abstract of Dissertation Presented to the
Graduate School of Argosy University-Orange County
In Partial Fulfillment of the Requirements for the
Degree of Doctor of Business Administration

THE EFFECTIVENESS OF THE SARBANES-OXLEY ACT OF 2002 IN
PREVENTING AND DETECTING FRAUD IN FINANCIAL STATEMENTS

by

Debra L. De Vay

2006

Chairperson: Dr. Ray William London
Committee: Dr. Judie L. Forbes
              Dr. Suzanne Holmes

Department: School of Business

The collapse of Enron, WorldCom, and other large corporations in 2001 and 2002 motivated Congress to pass the Sarbanes-Oxley Act of 2002 (SOX). The purpose of this legislation was to restore investor confidence in the United States stock markets, and to prevent and detect fraud in financial statements as well. This dissertation examines the effectiveness of SOX for the latter purpose of preventing and detecting fraud, using statistical enforcement data presented by the Securities and Exchange Commission, and financial statement restatement numbers published by the Huron Corporation. The two methodologies utilized to analyze the data were the unpaired t test and the chi square test. Surveys were also emailed to executives and certified public accountants across the country to extract opinions as to the effectiveness of SOX. The statistical analysis results displayed that in 61% to 65% of the data sets, the numbers prior to the enactment of SOX were no different than the numbers subsequent to the enactment of SOX. The majority of the survey respondents feel that the benefits of SOX are not worth the costs, it is not effective in the prevention and detection of fraud in financial statements, and that it should be modified, but not eliminated entirely. While some sentiment exists that SOX is salvageable if revisions are executed, both the quantitative and qualitative analyses indicate support of the null hypothesis, that SOX is not effective in the prevention and detection of fraud in financial statements.

DEDICATION

To my husband, Chris De Vay, who is my rock. And to my parents, Henry and Clara

Yabrof, who not only always told me I could accomplish whatever I set my mind to do,

but agreed to be my editors as well. And to the memory of my brother, Mark Yabrof,

whose encouragement and enthusiasm helped me through to completion.

ACKNOWLEDGEMENTS

I would like to thank my dissertation committee, Dr. Ray William London, Dr. Judie L. Forbes, and Dr. Suzanne Holmes, for their support and guidance throughout the dissertation process. I am forever grateful for their valuable suggestions and insights.

TABLE OF CONTENTS

CHAPTER ONE: THE PROBLEM

Fraud prevention and detection in financial statements is a very relevant topic in light of the financial scandals that have shaken the corporate world in the last several years, most notably in large, well-established companies such as Enron Corporation (Enron) and WorldCom. In response, the United Sates (U.S.) Congress passed the Sarbanes-Oxley Act of 2002 (SOX), officially legislation designed "to protect investors by improving the accuracy and reliability of corporate disclosures made pursuant to the securities laws, and for other purposes" (One Hundred Seventh Congress of the United States of America, 2002, p. 1). In order to complete this task to protect investors, the main goal of SOX is to prevent and detect fraud in financial statements, policed by the Securities and Exchange Commission (SEC). The proposed problem to be researched then is the determination of whether or not SOX, after being in place for over three years, has been successful and has actually been effective in preventing and detecting fraud.

Those affected by the passage of SOX are most notably public corporations that are obligated to comply with the many requirements of the law. The shareholders and investors that rely on the financial statements of the complying corporations will be positively affected by SOX, in the event that it fulfills its purpose of preventing and detecting fraud in financial statements. However, actions of the SEC in enforcing SOX will ultimately determine whether or not it has been suitably valuable.

SOX Background

Nothing has shaken the accounting and auditing professions more than the collapse of Enron and the resulting ban from auditing public companies placed on Arthur Andersen LLP (Arthur Andersen), one of the biggest and oldest accounting firms in the

1

U.S. The signal has clearly been sent of the need for change within the professions and throughout the audit function. Congress has reacted to the events with the passage of SOX, aimed at preventing another Enron scandal.

Enron, a Texas-based company, was formed as a result of the 1985 merger of Houston Natural Gas and InterNorth, two regulated natural gas companies. Eventually the company began an aggressive growth strategy with a developed "complex financial structure" (Reinstein & Weirich, 2002, p. 1). It was not successful at these endeavors, and the stock prices of Enron began to fall.

To make the stock offerings of the publicly traded corporation a more attractive investment, Enron began the development and use of special purpose entities (SPEs) as liability receptacles, which removed millions of dollars of debt from the balance sheet. SPEs are formed to operate as trusts for the parent company that developed them. The number of SPEs that Enron established at the time of the collapse of the company is estimated to be at more than 3,000 (Rossi III, 2002).

In 1999, Enron also set up several private investment limited partnerships, including LJM Cayman L.P. (LJM1) and LJM2 Co-Investment, L.P. (LJM2). The chief financial officer (CFO) of Enron, Andrew Fastow, was the managing member of the general partners at the same time that he was serving in the capacity as the CFO for Enron. These partnerships were used "in hedging transactions involving millions of shares of Enron stock and other company assets" (The Corporate Library, 2002, p. 1). In July of 2001, Fastow sold his shares of the partnership to a long time employee of Enron, Michael Kopper, who at the time reported to Fastow. The purchase price was alleged to be around $16.5 million (SEC, 2002), and Kopper resigned from Enron just prior to the transaction.

Then on October 16, 2001, the third quarter earnings for the year for Enron were made public, and the company acknowledged that it had recorded a $1.01 billion after-tax charge to the earnings in order to recognize "asset impairments, restructuring costs, and losses associated with certain investments" (Herdman, 2001, p. 11). Of this amount, $35 million worth of transactions involved LJM2. Also on this date, Enron revealed that it had reduced shareholders equity by $1.2 billion. Enron subsequently explained that this reduction was for "correction of accounting errors" (Herdman, 2001, p. 11). On October 24 of the same year, Fastow was replaced as the CFO of Enron and later terminated.

On November 8, 2001, Enron filed a Form 8-K with the SEC. The 8-K is considered a current events report that discloses important occurrences in a timely manner and which cannot wait until the next filing of the quarterly Form 10-Q or the annual Form 10-K. The 8-K that Enron filed revealed that it would restate the financial statements for the years ending December 31, 1997 through December 31, 2000, and also restate the financials for the quarters ending March 31, 2001 and June 30, 2001. These restatements resulted in a reduction of income of $569 million for Enron, which was 16% of the reported net income for those statements. Enron also warned investors not to rely on the financial statements for those time periods as previously disclosed, including those audited by Arthur Andersen, the independent external audit firm of Enron.

On December 2, 2001, Enron filed for Chapter 11 bankruptcy protection. With the filing of the Form 8-K, the SEC had already begun an investigation of Enron and the financials of the collapsing company. On November 29, 2001, the SEC investigation expanded to include the independent auditors of Enron, Arthur Andersen.

In 2002, many other companies followed in the scandalous footsteps of Enron. Such corporations included Adelphia Communications and Global, who filed for bankruptcy in that year, and WorldCom, whose internal audit discovered $3.8 billion of "miscounted" funds (Nationmaster, 2005, p. 1).

Congress had already begun to react in late 2001 and early 2002. Both the House of Representatives (House) Committee on Financial Services, headed by Congressman Michael Oxley, and the Senate Committee on Banking, Housing, and Urban Affairs, chaired by Senator Paul Sarbanes, were convening hearings with expert witnesses testifying as to the causes of the Enron debacle and other notable scandals. Both committees sent bills to the respective branches of Congress aimed at preventing and detecting the financial fraud that existed within failed as well as failing companies. These bills were eventually merged to create SOX.

Statement of the Problem

SOX was signed into law by President of the United States George W. Bush on July 30, 2002, "conferring much tougher regulatory and enforcement powers upon the U.S Securities and Exchange Commission" (Friedman, 2002, p. 1). It was "passed in haste and with regulatory zeal for the purpose of restoring the confidence of the investing public" (Keller, 2002, p. 1). Also, it is a "serious directive to raise significantly the standards of corporate transparency and accountability" (Friedman, 2002, p. 2). More than 12,000 publicly traded companies are subject to SOX, most of which are not large corporations.

The majority of SOX involves "regulation of the accounting profession and the auditing and financial reporting process" (Keller, 2002, p. 1). The provisions of SOX include such areas as limiting the services offered by independent auditors, documentation and audit of internal controls, corporate governance, personal accountability, enhanced disclosure, protection for whistleblowers, analyst conflicts of interest, and professional conduct for attorneys practicing before the SEC who represent publicly traded companies. SOX is "the most sweeping legislation affecting accounting, disclosure and corporate governance in a generation" (Keller, 2002, p. 1). As such, the importance that has been placed upon SOX by Congress and the investors indicates the significance that researching effectiveness of the legislation would be to the accounting community as well as to stockholders and the general public.

The study completed, described herein, of the effectiveness of SOX was undertaken not only to ascertain whether the legislation is fulfilling the purpose of preventing and detecting fraud, but also to establish if revisions are necessary to enhance the usefulness and to achieve the goals of the legislation. The study has also helped to determine if enforcing SOX is worth the other related issues that have arisen since its inception.

One such issue is the rising costs to corporations to comply with the legislation, especially the internal control standards of SOX. Some large U.S. companies are alleging that the accounting rules stemming from SOX that are "aimed at improving shareholder trust are hurting shareholder returns" (United Press International, 2004, p. 1). Another issue is the effect of the legislation on foreign companies. In 2003, 19 non-American companies were listed in the U.S. stock market, while in the year 2000, 50 were listed.

SOX "gets some blame since it forces foreign companies to meet more stringent reporting rules" (Rossant, 2004, p. 1). Also, smaller companies are electing to become private to avoid the regulations of SOX. "Since the new reporting requirements of the 2002 Sarbanes-Oxley Act took effect, the number of companies announcing privatization plans rose 30 percent from levels during the 16-month period before the law" (Bachman, 2004, p. 2).

Research Questions

The main research question encompassed by this study is whether or not SOX is effective in preventing and detecting fraud in financial statements. This would include several aspects of this question, one of which is whether or not SOX adequately addresses revision of the accounting and auditing processes by both public companies and external auditors in order to reasonably ensure discovery of fraud. Other aspects include whether SOX should be amended or revised to make it more effective or beneficial, and whether it should ultimately be discarded as ineffective.

Subsidiary study questions include whether or not the costs to comply with SOX are worth the results, and whether SOX is substantially different from previous studies that have been completed. In addition, the study will help clarify whether or not Congress is qualified to provide the solution to the current fraud situation, and if SOX will correspondingly result in the return of investor confidence in the securities market by providing adequate corporate transparency into the financial status of the target investment.

The response to the main research question of whether SOX is effective can be inferred by statistical analysis of judicial, legislative, and reporting enforcement actions prior to and subsequent to the enactment of SOX. The other questions require value judgments based on opinions as well as the statistical response to the main research question.

Assumptions

An assumption is not an assertion, but a statement to be tested for accuracy (Kaplan, 1998). SOX has been in effect for only slightly more than three years. One assumption made during this study involving the effectiveness of SOX in preventing and detecting fraud, is that a determination can be made at this time concerning SOX. Another assumption is that because of the notoriety of the recent corporate and accounting scandals, the interest in the study as a whole will be enhanced because of its relevance.

Other assumptions have been made in the course of the study as to the methodology of the research. One such assumption is that the enforcement and financial statement restatement data used in the study is adequate and relevant enough to answer the research questions and validate the conclusions, as well as be representative of the degree of effectiveness of SOX. Another assumption is that the analysis of this data provides enough consistent responses to point to a single result, and that the data analysis methods utilized in the study are the best available in interpreting the data to enable an accurate conclusion. If it were possible for the research to be ongoing, then additional data gathered and analyses completed may further support, or may even alter, the conclusions drawn in this study. This question will remain a task for subsequent studies on the topic.

The other category relates to the conclusions drawn from the research and the data analysis. One assumption is that these conclusions will be able to explain current outcomes and will be able to predict future outcomes. Also, the assumption has been made that the research is objective, and if any interpretations are made, they will be designated as such and explained from the research. Differing viewpoints will also be presented and explained in order to strengthen the conclusion drawn. Another assumption is that the readers of the research will draw the same conclusions as the ones presented, without bias or prejudice. This would indicate that these readers will interpret the results in the same way as those presented in order to reach a similar outcome.

Rationale and Theoretical Framework

"The problem of fraud is an ancient one" (Dushkin Online, 2000, p.1). The examination of SOX is therefore very relevant, considering that the legislation is the most recent response by Congress to this most ancient problem. The determination of whether or not SOX will be helpful in eradicating accounting and financial statement fraud will be of utmost interest.

Several remarkable theories exist concerning fraud in accounting and the presentation of the financial statements. Albrecht (2003) suggested that a good economy is actually hiding the problems that companies are experiencing, creating more of an incentive to "cook the books." Albrecht also stated the use of stock options as earnings for company executives is encouraging these executives to manipulate financial statements to result in higher stock prices. This tends to create a focus on the short term rather than the long term performance of the company. Albrecht also cited a 1998 Gallop Poll concerning corporate honesty, with the result that "50% of CFOs admitted having been asked to manipulate the books; 17% admitted they had" (p. 5). As far as auditors

are concerned, Albrecht observed that auditing does not bring in nearly as much revenue

as consulting does, which is why the certified public accounting firms were providing

several different varieties of services to their clients, including auditing, consulting, and

management information systems. As a consequence, auditors were becoming too

closely involved with their clients and participating in unethical practices to please them,

as Arthur Andersen did with Enron, a most profitable client of the firm. Traditionally,

certified public accounting firms "failed to take responsibility for fraud detection" (p. 10),

which is why SOX emphasizes more auditor involvement in fraud prevention and

detection.

Ballweiser (2002) explained some other theories. One theory was the normative

regulation theory of financial accounting, which guarantees "fairness for investors,

protecting them against fraud and exploitation" (p. 6), as well as providing a

comparability of financial statements. Ballweiser also stated the purpose of auditing is to

enforce accounting rules, again "guaranteeing fairness for investors" (p. 11).

Kwechansky (2003) talked about fraud itself. Kwechansky claimed that fraud has

been around a long time, virtually when "people began trading money for goods and

services" (p. 3), and also explained three types of fraud are to be considered, which are

investment fraud "by unscrupulous people" (p. 3); employee fraud in which employees

take inventory or money from the company; and corporate fraud, which has become

prevalent lately, in which the management of a company "defraud a company's

employees, investors, lenders and sometimes its customers" (p. 3). This third type of

9

fraud is the one which has come to the forefront in recent years, due to Enron, WorldCom, and other companies being involved in scandal.

Methodology

The study uses statistical methodology in order to examine the data that has been collected. The bulk of the data analyzed centers around enforcement actions begun by the SEC when financial statement fraud is detected. The difference between the mean number of enforcement actions realized before SOX was enacted and after SOX was enacted was tested using the unpaired t test. The chi square test was used as well to test the significant difference between the number of actions prior to SOX and the number of actions subsequent to SOX. These methods were utilized because they were determined to be the most effective methods to produce reliable results. The data was collected from reports by the Corporate Fraud Task Force (CFTF) presented to President Bush, statistics found on the SEC website, and the Reports on Administrative Proceedings published by the SEC.

The other statistical analysis used in the study involved the number of restatements of financial statements by public corporations. A comparison was made between the restatements that occurred prior to the enactment of SOX and subsequent to the enactment of SOX.

The methodology used throughout the study involved correlational research. Correlations were examined between various statistics and the occurrence of these statistics in relation to the enactment of SOX.

Delineation of the Research Problem

"The fall of Enron, WorldCom, and the others, while massive in size and shocking in scope, is nothing particularly new" (CFO, Magazine for Senior Financial Executives, 2003, p. 1). The main issue, then, which provides the basis for the research question examined by this study, is the determination of whether or not SOX has been effective against a problem that has existed for centuries, with little or no success experienced by the conclusions and provisions of previous studies.

Several commissions were organized in previous years for the purpose of completing studies on audit effectiveness and fraud in financial statements. The Commission on Auditors' Responsibilities (Cohen Commission) was created in 1974 to study auditor responsibilities as well as the perception of the public concerning auditor responsibilities. From October, 1985 to September, 1987 the National Commission on Fraudulent Financial Reporting (Treadway Commission) met for the sole purpose of identifying causes of fraud in order to prevent the occurrence of fraud. A subsequent study was called Fraudulent Financial Reporting: 1987-1997: An Analysis of U.S. Public Companies, which was concerned with fraudulent financial reporting and audit reform. In 1998, the Panel on Audit Effectiveness (O'Malley Commission) was created, which scrutinized the current audit model. The 1998 Blue Ribbon Committee on Improving the Effectiveness of Corporate Audit Committees (Blue Ribbon Committee) was not concerned specifically with fraud, but some of its conclusions could possibly lead to fraud prevention and detection. Despite these studies by very knowledgeable and qualified people, the collapse of Enron and other corporate fraud scandals still occurred.

11

Subsequently, the Enron scandal catapulted Congress into action to pass SOX in a timely manner, in the hopes that it would eliminate such scandals from occurring in the future. But the opinion has been expressed that the passage of SOX was "driven by the political need of Congress to appear to be 'doing something' in response to a crisis" (Berlau, 2004, p. 1). Other comments concerning SOX included that of T.J. Rodgers, chief executive officer (CEO) of Cypress Semiconductor Corporation, who decided "what prevents problems very simply is management choosing to run a clean ship, period" (Berlau, 2004, p. 3). This assumes management has good ethics and morals, for which point Dr. Constantine Konstans from the University of Texas at Dallas School of Management explained that "you can't legislate ethics or ethical behavior" (Miller, 2004/2, p. 1). Arthur Brief, director of the Burkenroad Institute of the Study of Ethics and leadership in Management at Tulane University, agreed, saying "you can't legislate morality" (Kurlantzick, 2003, p. 1). In conjunction with these thoughts, Toby Bishop, president and CEO of the Association of Certified Fraud Examiners (ACFE), explained that "one key to fraud prevention is to create an atmosphere where employees feel confident in reporting wrongdoing without being victimized, even if executives appear to be involved" (Business Editors, 2004, p. 1).

These thoughts lead to the question of the success of SOX so far in fraud prevention and detection, which has come under question. One such opinion states that "even Sarbanes-Oxley can be amended to provide greater transparency and accountability" (Miller, 2004/2, p. 2). According to a survey taken by the Management Barometer from the accounting firm of PricewaterhouseCoopers, "the percentage of executives with a favorable opinion of Sarbanes-Oxley dropped to 30 percent last month

[June, 2003], down from 42 percent when the same group was interviewed in October 2002" (PricewaterhouseCoopers, 2003, p. 1). While others, such as John Fogarty from the accounting firm of Deloitte & Touche and member of the American Institute of Certified Public Accountants (AICPA) auditing standards board, have expressed the opinion that "the Act [SOX] will help. It has a good system of checks and balances. However, 'tone at the top' [management ethics] is what counts" (Coustan, 2004, p. 4).

The notoriety and number of recent financial statement frauds that have occurred prompted the passage of SOX by Congress. Opinions have and will continue to differ as to its scope and effectiveness. This study was conducted to respond to the necessity of quantitatively measuring the success of SOX, not only to quell the debate as to its usefulness, but to also estimate the future worth of this and other similar legislation.

Statement of the General Research Hypotheses

In order to clarify the direction of the research on SOX, it is important to develop a research hypothesis, which is a statement that describes "the predicted results" (McMillan & Schumacher, 2001, p. 88). The hypothesis should also "state the expected relationship or difference between two or more variables" (McMillan & Schumacher, p. 89). The null hypothesis is considered the negative form of the research hypothesis (Kaplan, 1998, p. 247), while the alternative hypothesis states that the opposite of the null hypothesis is true. Two types of errors exist which are related to these types of hypotheses. A Type I error occurs when the null hypothesis is rejected when it is in fact true (McMillan & Schumacher). A Type II error occurs when the null hypothesis is accepted when it is in fact incorrect (McMillan & Schumacher).

For the research question of whether SOX is effective, the null hypothesis would be that SOX is not effective in preventing and detecting fraud. The alternative hypothesis would be that SOX is effective in preventing and detecting fraud. A Type I error would occur if the research led to the conclusion that SOX is effective, when it is not. A Type II error would occur if the research led to the conclusion that SOX is not effective when in fact it is.

The variables related to the hypothesis statements are in most cases either independent variables or dependent variables. The dependent variable is "a consequence of or is dependent on antecedent variables" (McMillan & Schumacher, 2001, p. 83). The independent variable "precedes the dependent variable" (McMillan & Schumacher, p. 83). For the research question related to the effectiveness of SOX in fraud prevention and detection, the independent variables would include the ability of the SEC to successfully enforce SOX; loopholes discovered within SOX; cost constraints in complying with SOX; the ethics of the executives within companies governed by SOX; the protection offered to whistle blowers; and the ability to amend SOX. The dependent variable would be the extent to which fraud can be prevented or detected by SOX.

Importance of the Study

The importance of this study in determining whether or not SOX has been effective in preventing and detecting fraud is mostly to determine if SOX is performing up to one of its main purposes. If the results of SOX are not sufficient, then the research will help to determine if it needs to be supplemented, or if an alternative solution needs to be implemented in its place. The study will also determine whether or not the SEC is capable of regulating the accounting field effectively through the use of SOX, and if indeed it is the appropriate authority to implement this or any accounting legislation. If the research demonstrates that SOX prevents and detects fraud, then the SEC acted appropriately. If the conclusion of the research is that SOX does not, then SOX should be amended in order to allow the SEC to properly implement it, or the possibility must be examined to allow the accounting profession to regulate itself and provide appropriate punitive measures.

Several audiences will find the study significant and useful. Certified Public Accountants (CPAs) will benefit from the study because it will assist them in assessing the appropriateness of SOX, and in determining whether other steps will be necessary in order to prevent or detect fraud more effectively. Other pronouncements, such as the Statement on Auditing Standards (SAS) 99, which addresses identification of fraud risks during audits, have already been developed to supplement SOX. In addition, as Joseph T. Wells, founder and chairman of the ACFE, explained, "The accounting profession needs to learn more about preventing fraud" (AICPA, 2004, p. 2). Assessing whether or not the directives of SOX are what is deemed necessary to prevent fraud will aid in the knowledge of CPAs in this arena.

Corporations will also be interested in the study and the results. SOX has caused additional spending by corporations in order to comply with the internal control standards imposed by SOX. According to Clayton and Mackintosh (2002), "officers of any organization – whether non-profit or privately held – may be affected by SOX's new standard of corporate conduct and the law's impact on penalties that can be threatened during an investigation" (p. 1). In a survey completed by PricewaterhouseCoopers, "the executives were, at best, lukewarm in their overall assessment of the law" (Berman,

DeValerio, Pease, Tabacco, Burt, & Pucillo, 2003, p. 1). In addition, "nearly two-thirds of executives saw the law as potentially damaging for themselves" (Berman, et al, p. 1). If the study discovers that indeed SOX is not preventing fraud, then it seems that corporations would be more than willing to lobby against it to be freed of its requirements.

Investors would also benefit by the study if it assisted them in determining whether or not SOX is protecting their interests. A poll of investors, done in January of 2004, "proves that investor confidence is closely aligned with companies' compliance with the Sarbanes-Oxley Act. Three in five investors believe that the law will help protect their stock investments" (SmartPros, 2004, p. 1). It would behoove the investors to read the study and be informed as to how effective SOX actually is in preventing and detecting fraud.

Definition of Terms

The following is a list of definitions of relatively unfamiliar terms that are mentioned and are relevant in the study. The intent of this list is to better inform the reader in order to enhance the understanding of the background of the study as well as the study itself.

American Institute of Certified Public Accountants (AICPA). The AICPA is the national organization for certified public accountants in America. The mission of the AICPA is "to provide members with the resources, information, and leadership that enable them to provide valuable services in the highest professional manner to benefit the public as well as employers and clients" (AICPA, 1995, p.1). The AICPA also establishes professional standards, and assists in enforcing these and other standards within the profession.

Audit Committee. The audit committee is a separate committee composed of members of the board of directors. The purpose of this committee is "overseeing and monitoring management's and the independent auditors' participation in the financial reporting process" (SEC, 2000, p. 2). When utilized properly, this committee plays a vital role in the integrity of the financial statements.

Auditing. Auditing is considered to be the main activity of the certified public accountant, and involves "an independent examination of the accounting records, the internal control system and other evidence…to support the expression of an impartial expert opinion about the reliability of the financial statements" (Aurora Public Schools, 2004, p. 2). Internal auditing is completed by employees within the company "designed to add value and improve an organization's operations" (The Institute of Internal Auditors, 2005, p. 1).

Bright line. This is a term used in not only the accounting profession, but in legal and other such professions. It is defined as "a clear distinction that resolves a question or matter in dispute" (FindLaw, 1999, p. 1). For accountants, the term is used mostly to describe certain standards and provisions.

Corporate Fraud Task Force (CFTF). The CFTF was established by President Bush on July 9, 2002, with the purpose of the CFTF being "to investigate and prosecute significant financial crimes, recover the proceeds of such crimes, and ensure just and effective punishment of those who perpetrate financial crimes" (Deputy Attorney

General, 2002, p. 1). Members are drawn from the Department of Justice, as well as federal, state, and local enforcement agencies.

Financial Accounting Standards Board (FASB). The FASB was instituted in 1973, and since then has been "the designated organization in the private sector for establishing standards of financial accounting and reporting" (FASB, 2004, p. 1). The AICPA and the SEC recognize the FASB as an official standard-setting body. The main mission of the FASB is to "establish and improve standards of financial accounting and reporting for the guidance and education of the public, including issuers, auditors and users of financial information" (FASB, p. 1).

Financial Statements. Financial statements are "the means by which accountants communicate information to users" (Needles, Anderson, & Caldwell, 1981, p. 1038). The statements are either audited or unaudited, depending on what is required of the corporation, and consist of the balance sheet, the income or profit and loss statement, the statement of cash flows, subsidiary notes, and detailed schedules, when necessary.

Forms 8-K, 10-Q, and 10-K. These forms are required of public corporations by the SEC, pursuant to Section 13 or Section 15(d) of the Securities Exchange Act of 1934. Form 8-K is filed with the SEC for current reports involving written communications related to business combination transactions; for soliciting materials and communications for tender offers; and for reports of nonpublic information required to be disclosed (SEC, 2004/4, p. 1). Form 10-Q is used to submit quarterly financial reports to the SEC, as well as transitional reports (SEC, 2004/6, p. 1). The purpose of Form 10-K is to submit annual and transitional reports to the SEC (SEC, 2004/5, p. 1).

Fraud. Fraud is defined as a "deception deliberately practiced to secure unfair or unlawful gain" (Legal Definitions, 2004, p. 1). It is also considered "an intentional misrepresentation of a material existing fact made by one person to another with knowledge of its falsity" ('Lectric Law Library, 2004/1, p. 1). Financial statement fraud is considered a "deliberate attempt by corporations to deceive or mislead users of published financial statements, especially investors and creditors, by preparing and disseminating materially misstated financial statements" (Rezaee, 2002, p.44).

Generally Accepted Accounting Principles (GAAP). GAAP are approved principles and provisions developed for the purpose of defining accounting and financial reporting standards. They come into existence in response to questions, and consist of either official pronouncements by authoritative bodies, or they evolve over time "when authoritative bodies fail to respond" (Delaney, Epstein, Nach, Budak, 2003, pp.1-2).

Going Dark. A company that goes dark can have no more than 300 to 500 holders of record, and less than $10 million in assets. Form 15 is filed with the SEC indicating that the company will no longer meet reporting requirements, but company control and ownership remain the same. The stock of the company will now be traded through the list of daily quotes of the National Quotation Bureau, which exists for companies which are no longer listed on any stock exchange (Norman, 2005).

Going Private. This particular operation involves a group or individuals that buy the outstanding shares of the stock of a company which is registered with the SEC. This process "alters control, capitalization and ownership of the company" (Norman, 2005, p. 4). Going private is more costly and more time-consuming than going dark, and when the transaction is completed, the shares of the company are no longer publicly traded.

Independent Auditor. The auditor is considered independent if the attest function can be performed by said auditor without bias or prejudice. Auditor independence is known as "the cornerstone of the auditing profession because it is the foundation for the public's trust" in auditing and auditors (Lindberg & Beck, 2004, p. 1). SOX limited the number of services that the auditor can provide to a client, thus redefining auditor independence.

Initial Public Offering (IPO). An IPO is defined as "the process of bringing private companies to the public market for the first time" ('Lectric Law Library, 2004/2, p. 1). It is the original offering of the stocks of the corporation in the stock exchanges.

International Accounting Standards Board (IASB). The IASB is an "independent, privately-funded accounting standard-setter" (IASB, 2005, p. 1). The IASB is based in London, England, and consists of members from nine countries. The main purpose of the IASB is to develop "a single set of high quality, understandable and enforceable global accounting standards that require transparent and comparable information in general purpose financial statements" (IASB, p. 1).

Materiality. The FASB defines materiality as the "magnitude of an omission or misstatement in the financial statements that makes it probable that a reasonable person relying on those statements would have been influenced by the information or made a different judgment if the correct information had been known" (Delaney, Epstein, Nach, Budak, 2003, p.9). Opinions differ as to the specific number or percentage at which an amount becomes material because the level is based on judgment and not on precise amounts.

Public Company Accounting Oversight Board (PCAOB). The PCAOB was established by SOX in 2002. It is a private, non-profit corporation, and the objective of the board is to "oversee the auditors of public companies in order to protect the interests of investors and further the public interest in the preparation of informative, fair, and independent auditors" (PCAOB, 2003, p.1).

Sarbanes-Oxley Act of 2002 (SOX). SOX was signed into law on July 30, 2002 in response to the collapse of Enron, WorldCom, and other large public corporations. The purpose of SOX is to improve investor confidence in the stock markets, and to decrease the incidence of financial statement fraud. SOX is discussed in greater length within the text of this study.

Self-Regulatory Organization (SRO). SROs are entities which regulate themselves without other authoritative bodies creating standards and rules for them. The securities markets in the U.S. are "grounded on the principle of self-regulation" (SEC, 2004/3, p. 11), established with the idea that "regulation is most effective when it is done as closely as possible to the regulated activity" (SEC, 2004/3, p. 11).

Special Purpose Entity (SPE). SPEs are entities that are "used to keep assets, liabilities, and commitments 'off the books'" (Delaney, Epstein, Nach, Budak, 2003, p.484). They are usually established as trusts or partnerships, and if the sponsoring corporation does not control the SPE, the financial statements of the SPE do not have to be consolidated into the financial statements of the sponsoring corporation. The assets of the SPE are also protected from bankruptcy and the creditors of the sponsoring corporation (Delaney, Epstein, Nach, Budak, pp. 484-485).

Tone at the Top. The tone at the top is an all-encompassing phrase which indicates the ethical and moral tenets of the upper management in a corporation, which, if successful, filter downward to the rest of the employees of the company. This "tone" can include "day-to-day fiscal prudence" (O'Sullivan, 2004, p. 2), as well as capital budgeting and ethical rules and standards. The "tone" also consists of stressing "the importance of honest reporting, transparency, and openness" (O'Sullivan, p. 2).

Transparency in Financial Reporting. Financial information should be transparent so that it "provides the complete reporting and disclosure of transactions, which portray the financial conditions and operational results of the company in conformity with GAAP" (Rezaee, 2002, p.26). Transparency allows users of the financial statements to "obtain the right information and ensure that financial information is factual and objective" (Rezaee, p.26). The more transparent the financial reporting is, the easier it is for users to "obtain and assess the nature of transactions and the quality of the related financial statements" (Rezaee, p.26).

Whistleblower. A whistleblower is "one who reveals wrongdoing within an organization to the public or to those in positions of authority" (The Free Dictionary, 2005, p.1). Section 806 of SOX provides for the protection of whistleblowers that are "employees of publicly traded companies and provide evidence of fraud" (One Hundred Seventh Congress of the United States of America, 2002, p.56).

Delimitations of the Study

A limitation is defined as a restriction, a shortcoming, or a defect (Dictionary.com, 2000). The limitations of the study are in many ways related to the assumptions and resultant of the assumptions. As such, the limitations may be separated into the same two categories as those listed in the assumptions section, gathering of the information and conclusions drawn from the research.

The first category involves the gathering of information. One limitation related to this is that SOX has been in existence for approximately three years. The information concerning the effectiveness of SOX may be limited, and therefore research may have to be expanded in order to collect enough data. Also, it is always a possibility that the data collected for analysis may not be representative of the effectiveness of SOX, or it may be very narrow in scope. Some bias may be involved in analyzing the data, although this is not usually the case with data analysis but can appear with qualitative analyses, such as surveys. In addition, the direction of the data may change with time, causing the current analysis to be invalid in predicting future outcomes.

The second category relates to the conclusions drawn during the study. As part of the previous study limitation, if it were possible for the research to be ongoing, then additional data gathered and the subsequent conclusions may change. This will make the conclusions more meaningful as they evolve with the experiences from the passage of time. Also, the research model may be too narrow or inappropriate, leading to inaccurate or inappropriate conclusions. The research may be too subjective or too narrow to provide a viable conclusion. In addition, the research could lead to an inaccurate conclusion, which would not apply to current situations. It may also occur that the readers will come to a different conclusion than the one presented due to conflicting interpretations. Because of the human experience and human nature, bias will exist in the readers, and this alone could cause different interpretations of the data, as well as the incidence of readers developing different conclusions than those presented.

Summary of the Problem

SOX came into existence as a rapid response by the U.S. Congress to the collapse of several large companies, as well as the effect they had on their investors and the general public. The main purpose of SOX is to improve investor confidence by preventing and detecting fraud in financial statements.

In the three years that have passed since the passage of SOX on July 30, 2002, the different sections of SOX have come into effect, both modifying the direction of the responsibility of corporations, as well as enhancing enforcement by the SEC of corporate fraud actions. The success of SOX in preventing and detecting fraud in financial statements is paramount to its success in improving investor confidence. Measuring this success, the focus of this study, is thus an important aspect relating to the determination of the effectiveness of SOX.

Outline of the Dissertation

In Chapter Two of the dissertation, the literature review, a discussion of the existing literature prior to the enactment of SOX will occur, and will include a summary of the literature and the value of the literature to the current study. Chapter Three will describe the methodology used to analyze the data collected for the study, while Chapter Four will detail the results and conclusions drawn from the data analysis. Chapter Five will summarize the problem and the conclusions, as well as present opportunities for further study on the subject of the effectiveness of SOX in preventing and detecting fraud in financial statements.

The next chapter, Chapter Two, discusses in detail the Congressional hearings, prior committee conclusions, articles, and books that influenced the enactment of SOX into law. Also discussed will be two studies and several opinions concerning SOX that have formulated subsequent to the passage of the legislation and the signing of SOX by U.S. President George W. Bush. The purpose of the chapter is to provide a literature base of SOX in order to better understand the foundation for, and consequently the intent of, the legislation.

CHAPTER TWO: THE LITERATURE REVIEW

SOX was implemented at a time of great investor uncertainty due to the recent collapse of Enron in October of 2001, as well as the similar demise of such companies as WorldCom and Global Crossing in early 2002. The main purpose of SOX was to restore investor confidence because "if investors don't have confidence or lose confidence in the integrity of the information they receive, they will flee the markets, and we all will pay a devastating price" (Sutton, 2002, p. 2). SOX was also designed to provide greater transparency of financial statements and disclosures reported by publicly traded companies. Generally, "the Sarbanes-Oxley Act is designed to help us ensure that our capital markets continue to be the envy of other nations" (Sarbanes, 2004, p. 1). Specifically, SOX was designed to put in place procedures to prevent and detect fraud, and to begin to reform the auditing profession as to its methodological and ethical approach to the audit of public companies. Debate has ensued as to the effectiveness of SOX in achieving the objectives of the legislation, considering whether it was devised too quickly by Congress to knowledgeably address the issues at hand. Also at issue are the costs required by public companies to implement the various sections of SOX, and whether the time and costs are worth the intended benefits of the legislation.

The main issue to be discussed in this study is the effectiveness of SOX in preventing and detecting fraud in financial statements. Various factors have contributed to prior incidences of fraudulent financial reporting, including deficiencies in the audit process, lack of appropriate corporate governance, and unethical management practices. The literature approaches each of these topics in detail, in preparation for the remainder of this study, which will assess their inclusion and effectiveness within the SOX legislation.

Passage of SOX

After Enron collapsed, the U.S. Congress took it upon itself to develop legislation to prevent and detect the type of fraud that brought down Enron and its outside auditor, Arthur Andersen. "Indeed the Enron debacle has become a poster child for a system that seems to be out of control" (Sutton, 2002, p. 1). The U.S. Senate Committee on Banking, Housing, and Urban Affairs, led by Senator Paul Sarbanes of Minnesota, and the House Committee on Financial Services, led by Congressman Michael Oxley of Ohio, each began the task of devising a bill to address the newsworthy issues brought to light by the filing of bankruptcy by Enron and the subsequent loss of pension funds suffered by its employees. The Congressional record is replete with discussions and debates concerning the issues at hand between experts in various fields as well as the members of Congress.

The Senate Committee Hearings

The Congressional record covering the "very intense set of hearings" (Sarbanes, 2004, p. 4) of the Senate committee detail the ten meetings it held with close to 40 witnesses to investigate the topic. The end result of these hearings yielded Senate bill 2673 (S. 2673) entitled the Public Company Accounting Reform and Investor Protection Act of 2002. The first hearing, which was held in February of 2002, covered the testimony of five former SEC chairmen, appointed by both Democratic and Republican presidents. Other witnesses included Paul Volcker, chairman of the Trustees of the IASB; three former chief accountants of the SEC; a former chairman of the FASB; Ira M. Millstein, who co-chaired the 1998 Blue Ribbon Committee; David M. Walker,

Comptroller General of the U.S.; Shaun O'Malley, chair of the 2000 O'Malley Commission; the current chair and former chair of the board of directors of the AICPA; chairman of the Auditing Standards Board (ASB) of the AICPA; Charles A. Bowsher, chair of the Public Oversight Board (POB) and former Comptroller General of the U.S.; and Harvey L. Pitt, then current chairman of the SEC.

According to Sarbanes (2004), "The hearings actually produced a remarkable consensus on the nature of the problem – inadequate oversight of accountants, the lack of auditor independence, weak corporate governance procedures, a stock analyst conflicts of interest…inadequate disclosure provisions…a grossly inadequate funding of the Securities & Exchange Commission" (pp. 4-5). Specifically, the major issues debated in the hearings were independence and involvement of the audit committees, a regulatory board for accountants to replace the now ineffective POB (Williams, 2002), rotation of auditors or audit partners, updated accounting rules (Levitt, 2002) written in a more timely manner, the company hiring of employees of the audit firm, the type and amount of non-audit services provided by the audit firm, management ethics, stock option expensing, and pay parity as well as increased funding for the SEC.

The House Committee Hearings

The Congressional record also documents the House Committee on Financial Services hearings on its bill, House of Representatives bill 3763 (H.R. 3763). The bill, ultimately titled the Corporate and Auditing Accountability, Responsibility, and Transparency Act of 2002 (CAARTA), began with an initial hearing on December 12, 2001, and continued until the bill went to the floor of the House in April of 2002.

The witnesses that appeared before the House committee included some of the same that appeared before the Senate committee, such as former SEC chairmen Richard C. Breeden and Roderick M. Hills; Lynn E. Turner, former chief accountant of the SEC; David M. Walker, Comptroller General of the U.S.; and Harvey L. Pitt, then current chairman of the SEC. Other witnesses included Joseph F. Berardino, managing partner and chief executive officer of Andersen Worldwide; William C. Powers, Jr., director of Enron; Barry C. Melancon, president and CEO of the AICPA; H. Carl McCall, comptroller for the state of New York; and Philip B. Livingston, president and CEO of Financial Executives International.

The President Weighs In

U.S. President George W. Bush (2002) had his own responses to the collapse of Enron, and to the type of reforming legislation he wanted Congress to devise. During his State of the Union address in January of 2002, Bush requested "stricter accounting standards and tougher disclosure requirements" (Bush, 2002/1, p. 7). In March of that year, Bush also requested that the system of personal accountability for corporate disclosures by officers and directors needed to be revised and improved (Pitt, 2002). On June 29, he advised U.S corporations that "no violation of the public's trust will be tolerated. The Federal Government will be vigilant in prosecuting wrongdoers to ensure that investors and workers maintain the highest confidence in American business" (Senate, 2002/5, p. 1). In July, while Congress was in the process of finalizing and passing SOX, Bush stated that "I challenge compensation committees to put an end to all company loans to corporate officers" (Senate, 2002/6, p. 11), and that "there can be no capitalism without conscience, no wealth without character" (Senate, 2002/6, p. 15). He also voiced his concerns about corporate ethics, stating that ethical standards should "be enforced by strict laws and upheld by responsible business leaders" and that "corporations should not be disconnected from the values of our country" (Senate, 2002/7, p. 84).

On July 30, 2002, President Bush signed into law H.R. 3763, "An Act to protect investors by improving the accuracy and reliability of corporate disclosures made pursuant to the securities laws, and for other purposes" (One Hundred Seventh Congress of the United States of America, 2002, p. 1). Upon signing the bill, the President supported its "tough new provisions to deter and punish corporate and accounting fraud and corruption, ensure justice for wrongdoers, and protect the interests of workers and shareholders" (Bush, 2002/2, p. 1).

Reform of the Auditing Profession

The auditing profession shouldered much of the blame for the lack of discovery of the fraudulent financial reporting that brought down Enron, WorldCom, and others. It did not help that staff at Arthur Andersen, the auditors of Enron, were caught shredding documents from the Enron file. "Auditors are expected to uncover and report to the public financial improprieties of the kind that existed at Enron" (Sutton, 2002, p. 3). Auditors should remember that in reality, their clients are the shareholders of the companies that they audit (House Financial Services Committee, 2002/4), and that the financial statements should be clear, concise, and disclose all the necessary information for shareholders and investors to make informed decisions concerning whether or not to purchase or sell the stock of the company. They should audit to produce a fair presentation of the financial status of the company, and not be so involved in the details of the audit procedures that the objective of reporting the overall financial condition of the company is lost. The challenge for SOX on this topic is whether the reforms that it promulgated for the auditing profession are enough to reassure the public that auditors are performing their jobs in such a way that they can assist in the cessation of fraudulent financial reporting.

Nearly all the witnesses, including Pitt (2002), Hills (2002), and Ruder (2002), in the Senate committee hearings agreed that a new independent oversight board was required to direct the audit firms to improve the quality and objectives of their audits. As to the issue of non-audit services provided to audit clients, most of the witnesses, such as O'Malley (2002), Sutton (2002), Walker (2002), and Bowman (2002), believed that non-audit services to audit clients should be limited, because not doing so induces a situation of conflict of interest, as well as some instances of auditors auditing their own work. Balhoff (2002) felt that too much limitation on non-audit services would hurt the smaller audit firms and the smaller companies, and Bowsher (2002) felt that no prohibition should exist against an audit firm offering non-audit services to its audit clients. In the meantime, Copeland (2002) cited studies that showed that "non-audit services do not impair auditor independence" (p. 1). Mandatory rotation of the audit firm was not agreeable to many of the witnesses, especially when studies were presented that showed that fraud is more prevalent in the first two years of a new audit firm because of the unfamiliarity of the firm with the client and the business processes of the client (Pitt, 2002). Rotation of the audit partners for the client seemed to be more of an agreeable solution (Copeland, 2002; Walker, 2002). The witnesses concurred that the hiring of an

31

audit employee by the client was a problem, and that a "cooling off period" needed to be observed before this should take place (Breeden, 2002; Biggs, 2002; Bowsher, 2002).

The House committee discussed many of the issues that the Senate committee discussed. Auditor independence was a point of debate, most importantly the extent of the non-audit services provided by auditors to their clients. Some, such as Roper (2002), felt that a ban on non-audit services to audit clients should be mandated, with any exceptions pre-approved by the audit committee. On the opposite side, Pitt (2002) emphasized that no direct correlation between consulting and audit failures exists, and that if an audit firm was restricted to audits only, it would be more dependent on audit fees and would suffer a loss of expertise. Most agreed that a new, strong accounting oversight board was necessary, and that a cooling off period should be required before an employee of an audit firm can accept employment from a client (McCall, 2002). In addition, auditor rotation or at least audit partner rotation was needed. Pitt also pointed out that auditors need to be appropriately trained, and that audit firms should not continue the practice of placing the least experienced audit staff on an audit, because they would be less capable of discovering fraud if it were indeed occurring.

The standards developed by the FASB are rules-based standards which encompass great detail, including exceptions and provisions. However, many Senate committee witnesses agreed that too many rules have been developed, and that "the system has been so precise so many times in saying what cannot be done that it has created an implication that whatever is not prohibited is permitted" (Hills, 2002, p. 2). These standards take years to research and develop, leaving companies to use antiquated rules or to fend for themselves before the standards are published. "It's the old adage of a

F.A.S.B. rule. It takes four years to write it, and it takes four minutes for an astute investment banker to get around it" (Hills, 2002, p. 2). Some who testified believed that the FASB should continue setting accounting standards, as long as it was independently funded and the SEC provided better oversight of the standards. Others felt that a new independent regulatory board should not only oversee the profession, but set the standards as well. Beresford (2002) cautioned that "Congress should not interfere with technical accounting standards" (p. 1), while Biggs (2002) agreed, saying "the private sector not Congress should set accounting standards" (p. 1). Some witnesses voiced their opinions on the need for principles-based standards, which encompass less of the procedures and more of the objective of the standard, while other witnesses, such as Lynn Turner (2002), former Chief Accountant of the SEC, said that "principles-based standards would not help" (p. 1). As in the Senate, most of the House committee witnesses agreed that accounting standards need to be more timely and more current. Chief Accountant of the SEC Robert Herdman stated that the FASB "needs to move more quickly with standard setting" (House Financial Services Committee, 2001, p. 32).

Fraud Detection During the Audit

Fraud detection by independent auditors is a viable requirement to emerge from the recent corporate scandals. Frieswick (2003) agreed that auditors must do more to discover fraud, which is what the public wants, and that audits decrease the incidence of fraud loss by half. In the meantime, auditor credibility has been called into question.

To detect fraud, Rezaee (2002) suggests that auditors practice professional skepticism during an audit, and that the audit personnel should be knowledgeable, skilled, and well-trained in order to recognize fraud and the risk of fraud. Auditors should also be wary of questionable accounting principles utilized by management, ensuring that the internal control system is sufficiently effective to prevent and detect instances of fraud. When fraud is suspected, the audit steps should be revised to obtain more reliable audit evidence, and include additional audit work closer to the end of the audit year (Rezaee). Mulford and Comiskey (2002) detail some of the keys the auditor can use to detect management manipulations of the financial statements. These keys include (a) the examination of percentage changes in accounts receivable and accounts payable that do not correspond with company and industry trends, (b) comparing inventory turnover and trends within the industry, (c) examining the controls over inventory, and (d) examining contingent liabilities for feasibility (Mulford & Comiskey).

Davia (2000) brings to light a major point relevant to fraud auditing which states that the majority of fraud occurrences are either not reported or not discovered. Davia has placed fraud into three groups. The first group involves fraud that has been discovered and exposed to the public. The second group is fraud that has been discovered by the victims, but the victims choose not to pursue the fraud for various reasons, and it thus does not become public knowledge. The third group is fraud that has not been detected and is known only to the perpetrators. Davia estimates that 20% of fraud is group one fraud, while 40% is group two fraud, and 40% is group three fraud. Davia continues by suggesting that detection of financial statement fraud can be discovered through fraud auditing, which is more concerned with the transactions that make up the balance in an account, and not just the balance itself, which is the emphasis of traditional auditing. Davia claims that without fraud auditing, "internal controls are not effective, especially when two or more perpetrators are involved" (p. 8). Proactive fraud auditing is difficult because "it requires auditors to institute search procedures to detect fraud in circumstances where there is not evidence per se to indicate that fraud may exist" (Davia, p. 14). However, most auditors are not trained in fraud auditing or fraud detection, and do not possess sufficient knowledge of evidence and its collection (Davia).

Davia, Coggins, Wideman, and Kastantin (2000) assert that proactive fraud auditing is not generally done because no generally accepted auditing standards or accounting principles have been developed to use as a guide for the auditors. The contention of the authors is that such standards and principles should be written so that auditors are prepared to prevent and detect fraud through such auditing methods (Davia et al). In investigating suspected fraud, interviewing of key employees is very important, as well as efficient note-taking and the recording of written statements, when necessary. Sufficient evidence must also be collected to pursue any action taken against the perpetrator or perpetrators (Davia et al.).

Dauberman (2004) suggests changing audit procedures in order to detect fraud. Audits should be conducted using the "bigger picture" (Dauberman, p. 8) perspective. It is difficult because "people have different values and what one individual considers wrong or unethical might be considered acceptable behavior to another" (Dauberman, p. 11). Also, some accounting systems are more susceptible to fraud than others. Employee fraud is usually for personal gain and does not result in fraudulent financial statements, while management fraud is usually for the purpose of falsely improving the appearance of the financial condition of the company, which is considered fraudulent financial reporting. Management fraud is also more difficult to detect (Dauberman). The three characteristics of fraud that are usually present are (a) perpetrators of fraud always have a reason for committing the fraud, (b) the opportunity to commit the fraud presents itself, and (c) in the mind of the perpetrator, the perpetrator can justify the crime (Dauberman). When the client has an effective internal control system, and the auditor can assess the risks of the client, understand the business and industry of the client, utilize analytical procedures, and redesign the workpapers of the auditor to help assess the risk of fraud, then the auditor can more effectively prevent and detect fraud in the financial statements of the client (Dauberman).

SAS No. 99

The auditing profession itself has issued a pronouncement concerning the detection of financial statement fraud during the audit, entitled Statement of Auditing Standard (SAS) no. 99, Consideration of Fraud in a Financial Statement Audit. It details the three conditions that are present when fraud occurs, which are (a) incentive/pressure, (b) opportunity, and (c) rationalization/attitude (Ramos, 2003). SAS no. 99 suggests that the auditor use professional skepticism when conducting the audit, setting aside any previous relationship with the client and the assumption that all clients are honest (Ramos). A brainstorming session is now required among the entire audit team in order to share information about the client and the industry of the client, and to establish the proper attitude and skepticism while performing the audit. Brainstorming should not be restricted just to the planning phase of the audit, but should also be applied during the information-gathering process as well as near the conclusion of the audit. In addition, SAS no. 99 "requires the audit team members to communicate with each other throughout the engagement about the risks of material misstatement due to fraud"

(Ramos, p.3). SAS no. 99 provides guidance on obtaining information to identify the risks of fraud by interviewing management and others in the company, performing analytical procedures, considering fraud risk factors, and obtaining information from other sources (Ramos).

SAS no. 99 states that the client may still retain a high risk of fraud even if all three conditions of fraud are not present. It details two instances that are always considered fraud risk, which are improper revenue recognition and the override of internal controls by management. A greater risk of client fraud caused by these two circumstances necessitates placing more experienced auditors on the job. Auditors are now required to consider the selection and use by management of accounting principles to assess risk, and to include an element of unpredictability in the audit procedures from year to year in order to surprise possible fraud perpetrators. The auditor should also examine accounting estimates and unusual transactions when establishing fraud risk. Sufficient evidence needs to be collected for high risk clients, especially if fraud is suspected, and the documentation must include all the fraud issues and procedures discussed previously (Ramos, 2003).

Cohen Commission

The Cohen Commission was an independent commission established in November, 1974 at the request of the AICPA. Its purpose was to "develop conclusions and recommendations regarding the appropriate responsibilities of independent auditors," and also to "consider whether a gap may exist between what the public expects or needs and what auditors can and should reasonably expect to accomplish" (American Institute of Certified Public Accountants [AICPA], 1977, p. xi). It met 66 days over several years, and reached its conclusions based on research projects as well as consultations with auditors, experts, and others involved in the audit process. The interesting point of this commission is that many of its recommendations re-emerged during the Senate and House discussions pursuant to the issuance of SOX.

The recommendations issued by the Cohen Commission began with the role of the independent auditor in society. The commission discovered that financial statement users expected auditors to "be concerned with the possibilities of both fraud and illegal behavior by management" (AICPA, 1977, p. xvii) by supervising management's actions as well as improving the quality and extent of the financial statements and the related disclosures. However, users felt that auditors were not meeting these expectations (AICPA). The commission also concluded that the financial statements were the responsibility of management, and that the responsibility of the auditors was to "audit the information and express an opinion on it" (AICPA, p. xvii). However, the commission established that the auditor "should not accept management's selection of an accounting principle simply because its use is not forbidden, and he [the auditor] should not accept management's rejection of a principle simply because it is not required" (AICPA, p. xviii).

In relation to the issue of fraud in financial statements, the Cohen Commission found that "significant percentages of those who use and rely on the auditor's work rank the detection of fraud among the most important objectives of an audit" (AICPA, 1977, p. xix). The detection of fraud as a major purpose of the audit has declined over the years, and the standards have tended to emphasize the limitations of the auditor to do so. However, the commission felt that it was important that the audit be designed to provide reasonable assurance that no material fraud existed in the financial statements. The independent auditor "has a duty to search for fraud, and should be expected to detect those frauds that the exercise of professional skill and care would normally uncover" (AICPA, pp. xix-xx). Also, the auditor should be capable of discovering any illegal or questionable acts by management in relation to the financials of the company, again by exercising professional skill and care (AICPA, p.xx).

Other recommendations discussed the need for the report by the auditor to "state its messages explicitly" (AICPA, 1977, p. xxiv), as well as the need for the auditor and the audit firm to avoid activities or associations that would "jeopardize or appear to jeopardize independence" or present a conflict of interest (AICPA, p. xxviii). The commission found that no justification existed for removing the standard-setting process from the accounting profession, and that the development of an organization separate from the AICPA to devise auditing standards "would involve economic and organizational problems" (AICPA, p. xxix). Oversight of the accounting profession should also remain within the profession, though "the profession's self-disciplinary efforts could be more effective and should be strengthened" (AICPA, p. xxix).

The Cohen Commission found that the users of financial statements expect somewhat different results than what are actually produced by the performance of the auditors. Generally the expectations of users are reasonable, however the gap is caused by the fact that "many users appear to misunderstand the role of the auditor and the nature of the service he offers" (AICPA, 1977, p. xii). Also, part of the problem rests with the accounting profession in that it "has failed to react and evolve rapidly enough to keep pace with the speed of change in the American business environment" (AICPA, p. xii).

Treadway Commission

The Treadway Commission was an independent committee sponsored and funded by the AICPA, the American Accounting Association (AAA), the Financial Executives Institute (FEI), the Institute of Internal Auditors (IIA), and the National Association of Accountants (NAA). It met from October, 1985 to September 1987, and the purpose of the commission was to "identify causal factors that can lead to fraudulent financial reporting and steps to reduce its incidence" (National Commission on Fraudulent Financial Reporting [NCFFR], 1987, p. 1). The Treadway Commission developed its conclusions and recommendations by examining research studies; consulting experts, such as the Chairmen of the SEC, the AICPA, the ASB, and the POB, as well as the Comptroller of the Currency and the Comptroller General of the U.S.; and reviewing case studies related to the topic of fraudulent financial reporting. Again, many of the recommendations of the Treadway Commission were cited by those testifying before Congress concerning items for inclusion in the SOX legislation.

Before listing the recommendations, the Treadway Commission warned that "no company, regardless of size or business, is immune from the possibility that fraudulent financial reporting will occur" (NCFFR, 1987, p. 6). Also, improvement is needed in all areas of the financial reporting process, and that "no one answer to the problem of fraudulent financial reporting exists" (NCFFR, p. 7).

Though the Treadway Commission focused mostly on corporate governance and management improvements, it also suggested reforms for the regulation of the accounting industry, including mandatory membership of audit firms in a professional organization that the SEC approved, and which provided peer reviews and oversight. The Treadway Commission also recommended that the ASB, which develops auditing standards, should be smaller and should be composed of equal numbers of public accountants and those not in public accounting (NCFFR, 1987).

COSO Commission

A subsequent study was completed to update the information on fraudulent financial reporting gathered by the Treadway Commission, and was also similarly referenced during the SOX Congressional committees. This study was called Fraudulent Financial Reporting: 1987-1997: An Analysis of U.S. Public Companies. It was commissioned by the Committee of Sponsoring Organizations (COSO) of the Treadway Commission, and it released the report in 1999. The COSO Commission developed several conclusions based on a comprehensive analysis of the occurrences of fraudulent financial reporting examined by the SEC from 1987 to 1997, and it voiced some recommendations as to audit reform.

The COSO Commission discovered that the majority (55%) of the fraudulent audit reports had an unqualified audit opinion, while most of the remainder of the reports revealed a substantial doubt by the auditor as to the going concern of the company (Committee of Sponsoring Organizations of the Treadway Commission [COSO], 1999). For auditors to better perceive fraud, the COSO Commission recommended reviews of interim financial reports in order to detect fraud at an earlier stage, while continuous auditing of the reports may also be an effective option (COSO). It also commented that "there is a strong need for the auditor to look beyond the financial statements to

41

understand risks unique to the client's industry, management's motivation towards aggressive reporting, and client internal control" (COSO, p. 9).

O'Malley Commission

In 1998, the chairman of the SEC requested that the POB create the O'Malley Commission, whose purpose was to examine the current audit model. The report and recommendations from the O'Malley Commission were published on August 31, 2000, and these results were based on analyses of current audit practices and standards; discussions with focus groups; results of surveys; and meetings with firms, regulators and professional bodies. In addition, O'Malley was selected as a witness to testify before the Senate committee hearings for the SOX bill.

The major recommendations included in the O'Malley Commission commence with the idea that "auditing standards should create a 'forensic-type' fieldwork phase on all audits" (Public Oversight Board [POB], 2000, p. x) for the purpose of detecting fraud in financial statements. Also, the ASB should create auditing and internal control standards that are specific and definitive, while the audit firms should place emphasis on the quality of the audits. The different regulatory bodies that oversee the auditing profession, including the POB, the AICPA, the SEC, and the SEC Practice Section (SECPS), should decide on a more unified system of governance over the profession, and should strengthen the POB to include disciplinary actions and special reviews. The SECPS must strengthen the peer review and the disciplinary processes, while the audit committees should pre-approve non-audit services provided by the external auditors that exceed a pre-determined maximum dollar amount (POB).

Corporate Governance and Management Reform

Improving corporate governance as well as the tone and ethics of corporate management is a major step to preventing and detecting fraud in financial statements. The issues to be addressed include a more involved and independent audit committee, improved internal controls, and a more ethical management team.

Corporate Governance Reform

The Enron collapse also represented a failure in the corporate governance of public and private corporations (Ruder, 2002), and more specifically, the audit committee made up of members of the board of directors. Also, at least a majority of the members of the audit committee should be independent, with some members having a financial background (Levitt, 2002; Millstein, 2002). Senate committee witnesses felt that the audit committee should have the ability to hire and fire the audit firm, and should also have better communication with the external auditors, the internal auditors, and various members of management (Litan, 2002; Teslik, 2002). As far as the board itself goes, testimony was presented that recommended that the CEO not sit as president of the board of directors, thus increasing the objectivity of the board (Seidman, 2002). The Cohen commission recommended as well that the board of directors hire the audit firm, and supervise its relationship with management. The board of directors and/or the audit committee must be more actively involved with the audit and its related disclosures (AICPA, 1977, p. xxix).

House committee witnesses also agreed that audit committees should be more involved, and should hire and fire auditors (House Financial Services Committee,

2002/4). In addition, directors on the board of public companies should adopt a higher standard of independence (House Financial Services Committee, 2002/4). Rezaee (2002) cites the existence of "business red flags" that signal the risk that fraudulent financial reporting could occur (p. 80). Such red flags include lack of vigilant corporate governance, oversight board, and audit committee, as well as weak internal controls.

However, simply reforming the corporate governance structure will not ensure fraud prevention. New standards of corporate governance mandated by SOX will be effective "only if a culture of compliance is established at the company" (Clayton & Mackintosh, 2002, p. 1). Berlau (2004) contends that in regard to an independent board of directors, "the data does not bear out that they look out more for shareholders' interests" (pp. 2-3).

Corporate Management Reform

Ruder (2002) felt that poor management and a flawed business model were the culprits behind the Enron collapse. "Managers of all of our corporations need to reject a philosophy that seeks to skirt the edges of accounting rules and instead the need to embrace a corporate culture of full financial disclosure" (Ruder, p. 6). In addition, Volcker (2002) felt that "management is pressured to present a good 'bottom line'" (p. 1), which causes management to devise earnings methods, some within the boundaries of the law and accounting rules, and some not. To remedy this, Senate committee witnesses testified that bonuses and incentives should not be tied to the bottom line. Reforms discussed included the prohibition of conflicts of interest by the CFO of the company or similarly placed financial officials without the advent of full disclosure of the situation to the shareholders (Breeden, 2002, p. 1). In the event of a restatement of the financial statements due to inappropriate financial practices, other Senate witnesses discussed having top management disgorge any profits made as a result of the original published statements (Breeden). "Don't pay executive bonuses based on inaccurate financial statements" (Kirtley, 2002, p. 1). To increase assurances of the fairness of the financial statements, testimony was presented to the Senate concerning the necessity for the CEO and the CFO to sign attestation statements as to the soundness and accuracy of the financial statements (Bowsher, 2002; Teslik, 2002; Turner, 2002).

Breeden (2002) felt that the code of ethics of a company should be included in the annual report, along with the disclosure of any overrides of the code. Langevoort (2002) advocated for victim liability of perpetrators of fraud, citing that the statute of limitations for fraud, which is one year after discovery, is much too short.

The red flags of Rezaee (2002) also apply to management. Too much emphasis on meeting earnings forecasts and expectations can lead to management devising whatever methods necessary to meet these goals. Also, management domination by an individual or small group is a red flag, as well as the existence of related party transactions that are material and unusual in nature. Significant turnover in accounting personnel and disputes with the external auditors also indicate fraud risk (Rezaee). In addition, Rezaee specifies that "the company is more apt to commit financial statement fraud if there is a strong motive and opportunity to do so" (p. 80).

Mulford and Comiskey (2002) advise that management can manipulate the numbers reported depending on the accounting principles selected and the way they are applied. The three such areas of application flexibility include (a) inventory costs, (b) software revenue recognition, and (c) goodwill amortization (which is no longer allowed) (Mulford & Comiskey). This is not considered fraudulent financial reporting, but when the decisions of management are not within the guidelines of GAAP, then it becomes fraudulent (Mulford & Comiskey). Mulford and Comiskey also indicate that manipulating accounting principles to meet or exceed desired earnings objectives is considered earnings management. Again, once this manipulation ventures outside the realm of GAAP, or the primary goal is to misrepresent the actual financial condition of the company and mislead the users of the financial statements, then it is considered fraudulent (Mulford & Comiskey). Other methods of manipulating the financial statements include recognizing premature or fictitious revenue, aggressive capitalization or amortization of assets, and misreported assets and liabilities (Mulford & Comiskey).

In order for management to combat fraud, Davia et al (2000) suggest the use of fraud specific internal control, which is defined as "a system of 'special-purpose' processes and procedures designed and practiced for the primary if not sole purpose of preventing or deterring fraud" (p. 98). The custodian and operators of such an internal control system must be competent, and the system itself should be tested periodically to ensure its effectiveness. Also, this type of internal control system would be specific to each company (Davia et al).

Other suggestions for detecting fraud include attempting to "create an atmosphere where employees feel confident in reporting wrongdoing without being victimized, even if executives are involved" (Business Editors, 2004, p. 1). According to Associate Professor of Accounting J. Edward Ketz, "despite Sarbanes-Oxley, we have a culture where accounting is viewed as a game...you're going to have managers who will try to do their best to try to look good via the accounting numbers" (Brand, 2004, p. 2). But

management reform is important because "what prevents problems very simply is

management choosing to run a clean ship, period" (Berlau, 2004, pp. 2-3).

Treadway Commission

As stated previously, the Treadway Commission was mostly concerned with

corporate governance and management reforms. The first recommendation of the

Treadway Commission emphasized the "tone at the top," which indicates the ethical and

professional environment developed by management that sets the tone for the rest of the

corporation (NCFFR, 1987, p.11). The right tone at the top can be established by (a)

identifying circumstances that can lead to fraudulent financial reporting, (b) maintaining

an effective system of internal controls over financial and other functions, and (c) the

enforcement of a comprehensive written code of corporate conduct (NCFFR).

Other recommendations include an internal audit department that is objective and

effective and an involved audit committee composed of independent directors which also

oversees the quarterly reporting process. Management must admit that it holds the

responsibility for the financial statements and the disclosures, and it should advise the

audit committee when and why it is seeking a second opinion on a corporate accounting

issue. New auditing standards are required that reflect the responsibility of the

independent auditor to detect fraudulent financial reporting; and improve audit quality by

adding, in addition to the established process of peer reviews, reviews of all first-year

audits for all public company clients new to the audit firm (NCFFR, 1987). Also, the

SEC should be given the power to impose stricter sanctions against perpetrators of financial statement fraud, found to be mostly top management, and should be awarded adequate funding and staff to successfully perform new and existing functions (NCFFR).

COSO Commission

Much of the findings of the COSO Commission involved management and corporate governance. Generally, the companies that were found to be committing fraudulent financial reporting were small companies, and they were not listed on either the New York or the American stock exchanges (COSO, 1999). Top management was involved in the fraud. "In 72 percent of the cases, the CEO appeared to be associated with the fraud" (COSO, p. 1). The board of directors and the audit committees of the fraud companies were not independent and appeared weak, and also, a large number of the companies were owned by the founders and the board members. Upon the commission of the fraud, the companies suffered such severe consequences as bankruptcy, change in ownership, and delisting on the national exchanges (COSO). The frauds that were committed were relatively large, considering the generally small size of the companies perpetrating the deceptions. Most of the frauds were committed over more than one period, and they usually involved the overstatement of assets and revenues (COSO).

Several conclusions were drawn by the COSO Commission in light of these findings. Small companies apparently could not afford to implement proper internal controls, or employ strong, ethical top management. Also, doubts about the going concern of the company may be an indicator of the occurrence of fraud in the financial statements. Boards of directors and audit committees should be more objective, and the selection by the board of a majority of independent members would assist in this goal (COSO).

Blue Ribbon Committee

The Blue Ribbon Committee, sponsored by the New York Stock Exchange (NYSE) and the National Association of Securities Dealers (NASD) was formed in September of 1998 and published the report in 1999. The report does not "focus on fraud per se, although many of our recommendations may reduce the possibility of fraud. The Committee's focus is on the large grey area where discretion and subjective judgments bear on the quality of financial reporting" (Blue Ribbon Committee, 1999, p. 2). The Blue Ribbon Committee interviewed many experts, including William T. Allen of the Independence Standards Board (ISB), William G. Bishop of the IIA, Kathleen Gibson of the American Society of Corporate Secretaries, Donald J. Kirk of the POB, Olivia F. Kirtley of the AICPA, and William B. Patterson of the American Federation of Labor - Congress of Industrial Organizations (AFL-CIO). The Blue Ribbon Committee also used the reports of prior committees, including that of the Treadway Commission, as well as the report on the Strengthening the Professionalization of the Independent Auditor, Report to the Public Oversight Board of the SEC Practice Section, American Institute of Certified Public Accountants from the Advisory Panel on Auditor Independence (1994). The Senate SOX committee also chose Millstein, who co-chaired the Blue Ribbon Committee, to appear as a witness and report on the findings of this committee.

Half of the recommendations of the Blue Ribbon Committee involved the composition and regulation of the audit committee. The committee felt that the audit committee of public companies with market capitalization above $200 million should be comprised solely of independent members. The committee defined independence for the audit committee members as "no relationship to the corporation that may interfere with the exercise of their independence from management and the corporation" (Blue Ribbon Committee, 1999, p. 10). The audit committee should be made up of at least 3 members, all of whom should be financially literate. The audit committee would benefit from a written charter, which would be reported in the proxy statement of the company for the annual meeting whether or not the audit committee had completed the responsibilities for the year as described in the charter (Blue Ribbon Committee).

The rest of the recommendations of the Blue Ribbon Committee concerned the relationship of the audit committee with the external auditor. The audit committee should be responsible for the hiring and firing of the external auditor, and should be responsible for communications with the outside auditor. The committee also recommended that generally accepted auditing standards (GAAS) be written that require the external auditor to discuss the quality of the accounting principles utilized by the company with the audit committee. In addition, the SEC should require that the audit committee include a letter with the annual reports of the company, detailing whether the outside auditors have discussed the quality of the pertinent accounting principles with the audit committee, and whether management has discussed the audited financial statements with the audit committee (Blue Ribbon Committee, 1999).

Quality of the Legislation

The quality of the legislation encompasses the issues of whether or not the legislation was devised and ratified too quickly, as well as if it or any other legislation would be enough to prevent and detect fraud. This issue calls to the very basis of this study, and the opinions offered here are noteworthy as to the effectiveness of SOX.

The judgments differed as to the speed with which the bill should have been written and enacted. Sarbanes, in presenting the bill to the floor of the Senate, reiterated that "we sought to do a very thorough and careful job in developing this legislation" (Senate, 2002/1, p. 8). Copeland (2002) and Whitehead (2002) cautioned Congress not to react too quickly, and to "wait with legislation for the self-cleaning process" (Whitehead, p. 1). However, Peters (2002) and Pitt (2002) both agreed that major legislative change should be completed as rapidly as possible.

House Subcommittee Ranking Member Paul E. Kanjorski also addressed the timing of the legislation, pleading, "Don't rush the legislation" (House Financial Services Committee, 2002/1, p. 1). Marc Lackritz, president of the Securities Industry Association, echoed this same sentiment (House Financial Services Committee, 2002/2), while Melancon felt that Congress should not over-legislate or over-react (House Financial Services Committee, 2002/2, p.25). Joseph V. Del Raso, Esquire, Partner at Pepper Hamilton LLP, expressed reservations by saying that "Congress should be careful not to fix things that are not broken" (House Financial Services Committee, 2002/3, p. 1). Walker explained that it is "better to get it right than do it fast, but there is a need for expeditiousness, especially in connection with the audit area" (House Financial Services Committee, 2002/4, p. 22). And Damon Silvers, associate general counsel of the AFL-CIO, warned that "Congress needs to take action, but it must be effective" (House Financial Services Committee, 2002/4, p. 40).

Some Senate committee witnesses felt that legislation would not be enough to prevent and detect fraud. As Williams (2002) testified, "Ultimately any system can be subverted" (p. 3). Williams went on to say that "in the final analysis, the system works as it should only when all the players honor the spirit as well as the letter of the law" (p. 3). Ruder (2002) added to this idea by testifying that "I do not believe its possible for the government to legislate good morals, and I believe efforts to do so may stifle innovation. Congress should not legislate in this area" (p. 7). Millstein (2002) asserted that "the great conundrum is that notwithstanding all our efforts for corrections, ultimately, to a considerable degree, we are left to rely on the integrity of individuals" (p. 11). Teslik (2002) answered this by asserting that "we cannot rely on people's honor or professionalism" (p. 1).

On the floor of the Senate, Sarbanes declared that "we are anxious to reassure accountants all across the country that we think that this legislation will help bring the profession back to the standards that marked it at an earlier time" (Senate, 2002/1, p. 42). Other senators discussed the merits of the bill during the Senate sessions. Senator William P. Gramm of Texas responded by emphasizing that "there are many good things in the Sarbanes bill...I do think it can be improved. I think it legislates too much. I think it does one-size-fits-all mandates" (Senate, 2002/1, p. 24). Senator Michael B. Enzi of Wyoming, the only CPA in the Senate, also reacted, saying, "Make no mistake about it, this legislation is federalization of the accounting industry" (Senate, 2002/1, p. 27). Senator Bryon L. Dorgan of North Dakota expressed the opinion that "we can change the law, but if we do not have a tough, no-nonsense regulator, then it will not work" (Senate, 2002/1, p. 26). Senator Paul Wellstone of Minnesota affirmed that "Sarbanes has dealt with the underlying structural issues so we can prevent this from happening again" (Senate, 2002/2, p. 4). Wellstone also claimed that "this is the best of government oversight. I am very proud to support this legislation" (Senate, 2002/8, p. 5). Senator Carl Levin of Michigan stressed that "as strong as it is, the Sarbanes bill would benefit from a number of strengthening measures" (Senate, 2002/3, p. 2), while Senator Jack Reed of Rhode Island proclaimed, "I rise in strong support of the Sarbanes legislation" (Senate, 2002/4, p. 1).

Other Senate opinions were more cautionary. Senator Richard Santorum of Pennsylvania worried about small businesses, saying, "To put these kinds of rules and regulations in place for these small companies is going to be very expensive, very onerous, and make it very difficult for them to conduct business" (Senate, 2002/6, p. 19). Senator George Allen of Virginia cautioned that "in our effort to reform, we must not enact measures that stifle innovation and endanger the American entrepreneurial spirit" (Senate, 2002/7, p. 27). Senator Joseph R. Biden, Jr. of Delaware was also guarded, saying that "we have had occasion to overreact. We have found sometimes that the cure is worse than the disease," but concluded by saying "there is a real balance that Sarbanes has struck" (Senate, 2002/7, p. 32). The concern voiced by Senator Robert Bennett of Utah involved the accounting profession itself, and insisted that "the one thing that we should be most careful of, however, is to avoid having Congress set the accounting rules…Past history tells us Congress can act in a hurry but repent at great leisure" (Senate, 2002/7, pp. 47-49). These senators and others, including Senator Dianne Feinstein of California, Senator Orrin Hatch of Utah, and Senator Christopher Dodd of

Connecticut, felt the bill was not the final answer to the issues of fraud and investor confidence, but that it was "a critical piece of the overall effort" (Senate, 2002/7, p. 99).

Comments on the floor of the House included those by Congressman Charles F. Bass of New Hampshire, who said that "we should be very careful not to stifle capitalism in this country" (House of Representatives, 2002/1, p. 3). Congressman Clifford Stearns of Florida asserted that such changes needed to be made to the accounting profession because "the current financial reporting system has to be changed...it was developed in the 1930s...for the Industrial Age" (House of Representatives, 2002/1, p. 10). Kanjorski added that "we have not solved everything, by a long shot...But I believe that we have now put teeth into the accounting process" (House of Representatives, 2002/2, p. 5). And Congressman Margaret Roukema of New Jersey said "it is very good, but not perfect" (House of Representatives, 2002/2, p. 15).

Miller (2004/2) felt that SOX was not going to make much of a difference because "you can't legislate ethics or ethical behavior, and if people are bent on putting their own interests above those of the organization, you'll still have problems" (p. 1). Kurlantzick (2003) agreed, commenting that "you can't legislate morality" (p. 1). Rezaee (2003) emphasized that "it [SOX] does not address the core problem of auditors' conflicts of interest and has narrow implications because it applies to only publicly traded companies and their associations" (p. 20). The question also arises, "will the total collapse of investor confidence in our markets and trust in the private sector ever be rebuilt?" (CFO & Magazine for Senior Financial Executives, 2003, p. 1). Ketz asserts that three big obstacles to preventing and detecting fraud are still prevalent, and they are (a) stock options, (b) auditors still viewing themselves as working for management and not for the shareholders, and (c) boards of directors still rubber stamping the desires of management (Brand, 2004). Many consider SOX as representing "among the most significant changes to financial reporting since the SEC Act of 1934" (Pellet, 2003, p. 1), but companies are still spending a lot of money to be in compliance with section 404 of SOX, and Berlau (2004) claims that it adds "very little benefit to shareholders" (p. 1). The number of companies that became private entities increased 63% in 2002 from 2001, possibly because of the costs and complexities of SOX (Berlau, p. 3). Harrington (2003) asserted that "Sox is much more than a piece of legislation. It's a whole new way of thinking about corporate governance and CPAs and their employers must treat it as such" (p. 4). Robert Kerstein, an accountant and financial historian, claimed that "history just repeats itself – fraud and greed" (Scherer & Francis, 2002, p. 2).

One Year Later – The Coates Study

SOX was one year old on July 30, 2003. At this date, studies were completed and commentary written concerning the effectiveness of SOX up to that point in time. Among these was the Coates study (Coates, 2003), whose main purpose was to examine the impact of SOX on the corporate ethical climate after one year. Because the ethics of the management team dictates the probability of fraud within the company, this study is relevant to the issue of the effectiveness of SOX on preventing and detecting fraud.

Coates (2003) used surveys as the method selected to gather data on employee perceptions of ethics in the corporation in 2003 versus 2000. The interpretation of the findings suggests that management appears to have become more ethical in 2003 as opposed to 2000. Also, because more formal ethics programs have been developed in corporations, misconduct is being reported more frequently, and larger companies show a higher percentage of the reporting of misconduct than do smaller companies (Coates). Nearly one-third of the respondents claim that questionable practices still exist, and that younger managers under the age of 30 with less than three years at the company are more likely to succumb to pressure to compromise their ethical standards. Also, less than 58% of the employees that have reported misconduct are satisfied with the responses by their companies to the misconduct reporting. Another aspect of the survey resulted in the finding that SOX has been costly for the companies surveyed, but that management does expect annual costs of compliance with SOX to remain the same or even decrease over time (Coates).

Coates has incorporated recommendations into the study. These recommendations include that shareholders should demand more disclosure and more relevant information; employees should demand more corporate responsibility; retirement investments should not be placed solely into the stock of the company or into any one single stock; CEOs need to be reminded that when the company goes public, it now belongs to the shareholders; and business ethics courses should be given to management periodically as well as become part of the curriculum at colleges and universities (Coates, 2003).

Two Years Later

The two year anniversary of SOX, July 30, 2004, also produced commentary and opinion as to the progress of the legislation. The House Financial Services Committee even held a special hearing to interview witnesses heard during the 2002 gathering of data prior to the development and passage of SOX. This information is relevant to the current perception of the effectiveness of the legislation.

The House Finanical Services Committee

The witnesses that the House interviewed at the two year anniversary of SOX included James H. Quigley, CEO, Deloitte & Touche; Mitchell H. Caplan, CEO, E*TRADE Financial; Roderick M.Hills, former Chairman of the SEC; Del Raso; and Richard Trumka, Secretary-Treasurer of the AFL-CIO. Oxley also made statements at this time. One of the major issues discussed during this hearing was the costs of implementing SOX, and if the perceived benefits of SOX are worth the costs.

According to Oxley (2004), the returns on SOX two years later were positive, even though no law will stop all fraud from occurring. Large costs are involved in implementing the provisions of SOX, especially Section 404 concerning internal control. But the comment by Oxley confirmed that "if companies find that certain mandates like the internal control standard are particularly costly, maybe that's because they were deficient in the particular area" (p. 1). Oxley also cited recent surveys, saying that "a majority of corporate directors believe SOX has had a positive impact on their companies and their boards" (p. 2).

Quigley (2004) agreed that progress is being made because of SOX. Audit committees are better prepared, and are increasing the amount of time involved as well as their overall effectiveness. Quigley also cited a survey, which was completed in January of 2004 and included selected Fortune 1000 companies that were clients of Deloitte & Touche. This survey showed that the number of annual audit committee meetings has increased by more than 50% since the passage of SOX (Quigley). However, Quigley felt that "further legislation and regulation could undermine SOX's intentions" (p. 8). Also,

Quigley stated that "we should give SOX time to work and to reach its full potential" (p. 19).

Caplan (2004) and Del Raso (2004) made similar comments concerning the complete prevention and detection. Caplan asserted that "there is also no way to completely eliminate mistakes or scandal from business" (p. 12). Del Raso was more explicit, saying that "in the end you can't legislate personal character and morality. But if it continues to have the desired effect – the ongoing restoration of public confidence in the capital markets – then SOX has indeed met its objectives" (p. 1).

Trumka (2004) further addressed the issue of the costs incurred by companies when implementing SOX. The reaction by Trumka was that "there is ample evidence that incurring these costs is better than the alternatives" (p. 3). Trumka also responded to the report that some small public companies have made the decision to become private because of the costs and complexities of compliance with SOX. "We believe that many of these companies should never have been public in the first place" (Trumka, p. 3). But Trumka asserted that the job is not complete because several corporate governance issues have still not been addressed, such as continued defrauding of the investing public due to legal system deficiencies, and the lack of disclosure of executive compensation. The expensing of stock options is still an open issue as well (Trumka).

Hills (2004) added to the comments by saying that SOX has already had a beneficial impact on corporate governance. Auditors must communicate with the audit committees, and SOX prevents the audit committees from simply complying with management concerning the engagement of the audit firm. Also, the cost is worth the effort of complying with SOX, and the chief accounting officers of three very large corporations feel that compliance with the internal controls required by SOX is well worth the effort. "Many of these companies are putting in place internal controls that should always have been there" (Hills, p. 1). As to the companies that are staying private to avoid compliance with SOX, Hills concluded that "maybe they are not ready to have their stock traded" (p. 1). But Hills still claimed that "it is too early to conclude that all is fine" (p. 1).

Other Comments

Miller (2004/1) also commented on SOX two years later. Miller asserted that the legislation "brought an end to decades of self-regulation for the accounting profession" (p. 1). SOX also holds accountable executives who have committed financial statement fraud with more stringent penalties, and that it "helps to close loopholes that have allowed for continued offenses in America's corporate community" (Miller, p. 1). Miller commented that risk is inherent in the investing process, and that risk is part of the successful functioning of the capital markets. Miller added that "Congress should, however, ensure that every corporation plays by the rules, that all investors have access to the reliable information needed to make prudent decisions, and that each party who violates our securities laws is held accountable" (p. 1).

Sarbanes (2004) was also quite optimistic at the two-year mark of the legislation. The SEC is "newly invigorated," and is implementing various segments of SOX (Sarbanes, p. 5-6). However, Sarbanes did concede that "the SEC will continue to confront for some time the deep seeded problems of accounting, auditing and corporate governance that have taken such a heavy toll on our markets in recent years" (p. 6). The work is still not done.

The Zhang Study

In February of 2005, Zhang (2005) completed a dissertation entitled *Economic Consequences of the Sarbanes-Oxley Act of 2002*. The purpose of this study was to analyze the market reactions to the passage of SOX in order to quantify private benefits and costs of SOX. Citing the premise that stock prices reflect all the private benefits and costs of SOX, Zhang examined the changes of the market index during the process of enacting SOX and found that "the cumulative abnormal return around all the significant rulemaking events related to SOX is significantly negative" (p. 2).

The conclusions that Zhang (2005) produced as a result of the study are not complimentary to SOX. One such outcome suggested that "investors consider the Act [SOX] to be costly and/or the information conveyed by the passage of the Act to be bad news for business" (p.36). Another finding revealed that the restriction of nonaudit services required by SOX as well as the internal control reforms delineated in Section 404 of the legislation are both costly. Zhang also discovered that public companies with weak corporate governance were not benefiting from the regulations of SOX, which "significantly challenges the value of SOX, as it is primarily characterized as legislation 'improving' corporate governance and increasing shareholder value" (p.36).

Issues Relevant to SOX

Many experts agree, in testimonies, studies, writings, and research conducted over the last 30 years, that certain standards, procedures, and ideas must be implemented by corporate management, corporate boards and committees, and independent auditors in order to attempt to prevent and detect fraud in financial statements. These issues include (a) a strong oversight board for the auditing profession, (b) more timely and effective

60

auditing and accounting standards, (c) the exclusion of non-audit services to audit clients to protect auditor independence, (d) independent audit committees, (e) increased responsibility of the audit committees, (f) management ethics reforms, and (g) whistleblower reforms.

The opinions, conclusions, and recommendations presented in this chapter comprise the wealth of material from which the Senate and the House could draw in order to produce SOX, and to devise a very effective piece of legislation. Whether or not these Congressional bodies were successful will be the subject of the following chapters. The next chapter, Chapter Three, will discuss the methodologies and procedures utilized by this study to analyze the effectiveness of SOX in the prevention and detection of fraud in financial statements.

CHAPTER THREE: METHODOLOGY AND PROCEDURES

In designing the methodology to provide evidence in order to predict the ability of SOX to effectively prevent and detect fraud, a quantitative approach was selected to eliminate as much personal bias and opinion as possible. Based on the difficulty of obtaining raw data from the SEC and other government sources, data was examined as reported by these government agencies.

Four types of reported data were thus used in the analysis in order to compensate for the lack of raw data. The first two data groups are comprised of SEC enforcement statistics as well as data from the CFTF first and second year reports to the President. The third data group is from a report by a company called Huron Consulting Group, Inc. (HCG), formed in 2002 by former Arthur Andersen partners and providing a "variety of financial and legal consulting services to corporate clients that are in financial distress" (Hoover's Inc., 2005, p.1). The HCG report enumerates financial statement restatements. The final data group consists of statistics from the SEC Reports on Administrative Proceedings (see Appendixes B, C, D, and E).

Two types of statistical testing were used to analyze the data. The unpaired t test, a parametric statistical analysis which provides a test of means, was one test used to analyze these four types of data. The analysis was conducted by comparing the means of the statistics reported prior to the passage of SOX as against the means of the statistics reported subsequent to the passage of SOX. The second test was the chi square non-parametric test of statistical significance. Post-SOX data was compared to pre-SOX data to determine if a statistically significant difference exists between them.

The hypotheses to be supported by the data analysis, in encompassing the effectiveness of SOX, delineate the adverse as well as the constructive effects of SOX on preventing and detecting fraud. The null hypothesis states that the passage of SOX causes no difference, either positively or negatively, as to the prevention and detection of fraud, while the alternative hypothesis reflects that SOX does make a difference, whether positively or negatively, in the prevention and detection of fraud in financial statements. The initial assumption, considering the futile attempts at fraud elimination from other studies and legislation, was that the null hypothesis would be supported by the data.

Research Questions

As discussed in Chapter One, several questions can be addressed through the indicated research. The main question, of course, concerns the effectiveness of SOX to prevent and detect fraud in financial statements. This encompasses many aspects of the legislation, including its ability to provide for better results than previous studies that have been conducted, and to also present viable industry recommendations designed to combat the problem. Regulations have been developed by the accounting profession with the intention of addressing fraud in financial statements, including SAS 82, Consideration of Fraud in a Financial Statements Audit. These actions have not been successful, which begs the question as to whether or not it is deductively possible that SOX will be able to prevent and detect fraud where other regulatory and legislative bodies of work have not. And if not successful, then the possibility exists that SOX should be revised or amended, or should be discarded entirely as a respectable but failed attempt.

SOX has been determined to be expensive and time-consuming to implement by the corporations affected, especially Section 404 of the legislation (see Appendix A, a summarized version of SOX) as it relates to internal control within the company. This sentiment is voiced by Independent Community Bankers of America (ICBA) president and CEO, Camden R. Fine, who explains that "it is clear from the survey that complying with Section 404 of Sarbox [SOX] is a major financial burden for publicly held community banks" (PR Newswire Association LLC, 2005/1, p. 1). This research should help to determine if the expenditures of cost and time are actually worth the perceived results.

One of the main goals of the authors of the SOX legislation was to improve investor confidence in the securities market and to provide better investor protection by increasing corporate transparency of financial statements (One Hundred Seventh Congress of the United States of America, 2002, p. 1). The research will address the achievement of SOX in attaining this goal as well.

Research Methodology and Approach

Because of the use of reported data, as described above, the best approach in developing a design for the research is the use of a correlational design. In correlational research, the researchers "do not (or at least try not to) influence any variables but only measure them and look for relations (correlations) between some set of variables" (StatSoft, 2003, p. 1). In experimental research, on the other hand, researchers "manipulate some variables and then measure the effects of this manipulation on other variables" (StatSoft, 2003, p. 1). In this study, the data was to be examined as reported and not manipulated; therefore, this demanded that the correlational design be used to develop the relationship among the four types of reported data analyzed as well as the relationship of each to the effectiveness of SOX. Thus this method was determined to be the most efficient method of establishing support for either the alternative hypothesis or the null hypothesis.

The strategy of the study is to determine from the data if more or less SEC and judicial actions have been implemented subsequent to the enactment of SOX in July of 2002, and if more or less restatements of financial statements have been introduced since the legislation went into effect. The correlation in this instance is that if more judicial actions have been implemented, then the detection of fraud is improved. However, this also means that the prevention of fraud has not improved. If more restatements have been introduced, then again detection has improved, but prevention has not. Conversely, if fewer judicial actions have been implemented, then either prevention has improved or detection has not. The same can be said for the restatements.

Research Design

The nature of the research in this study, which consists of analyzing judicial actions and reports which are reactionary to the enactment of SOX, does not lend itself to traditional methods of raw data collection, either through subject studies or the numerical assignment of source documents. Subject studies are not practicable in this research, and source documents, mostly in the possession of government agencies, are not easily accessible. For this reason, the four types of reported data listed previously have been used to provide support for the research hypotheses, and to specifically determine whether or not the passage of SOX results in a difference, either positively or negatively, in the prevention and detection of fraud in financial statements.

The data analysis methods utilized are not only based on the correlational design, as explained in the prior section, but also on the reported data used. The reported data is numerical in nature, and encompasses the quantity of judicial actions, incidents, and restatements prior to the enactment of SOX in July of 2002, and subsequent to the enactment of SOX (as displayed in Appendixes B, C, D, and E). The independent variables identified in the data analysis section of the study are the time periods of interest, which are the months and years prior to the enactment of SOX, and the months and years subsequent to the enactment of SOX. The dependent variables are the occurrences within each category which fall within one of the two specified time periods. The most effective method to analyze the differences or similarities between the two sets of dependent variables is a test of means. An unpaired t test was used as the test of means. A test of significant difference is also useful in analyzing the data, so therefore the chi square test was run to compare the two groups of information.

The data itself was collected from the Internet, using appropriate key words to locate the type of data required. The SEC website, www.sec.gov, proved to be a very useful source of information for SEC enforcement actions and proceedings. Once this website was located, the "Enforcement" section of "SEC Divisions" was selected off the home page. This produced the page at the www.sec.gov/divisions/enforce.shtml address, and each of the categories, "Federal Court Actions", "Administrative Proceedings", "ALJ [Administrative Law Judges] Initial Decisions & Orders", "Commission Opinions", and "Trading Suspensions" were in turn selected from this page. This produced the respective web pages of www.sec.gov/litigation/litreleases.shtml, www.sec.gov/litigation/admin.shtml, www.sec.gov/litigation/aljdec.shtml, www.sec.gov/litigation/opinions.shtml, and www.sec.gov/litigation/suspensions.shtml. These pages listed the litigation that had occurred in the years between 1995 and 2005, which were then counted to decipher the amount in each fiscal year from October 1st to September 30th. These counts were used in the analysis process.

For the reports from the CFTF, the key words "Corporate Fraud Task Force" were typed into the MSN search engine. The website, www.usdoj.gov/dag/cftf, appeared as the main listing for these key words. Once at this website, several listings were presented from which to choose, one of which was *First Year Report to the President: Corporate Fraud Task Force, July 22, 2003*, at www.usdoj.gov/dag/cftf/first_year_report.pdf, which was selected for SEC enforcement action data from the fiscal year 2000 to June 30, 2003. Another listing chosen was *Second Year Report to the President: Corporate Fraud Task Force, July 20, 2004*, at www.usdoj.gov/dag/cftf/2nd_yr_fraud_report.pdf, which was selected for SEC enforcement action data from the fiscal year 2001 to June 30, 2004.

The HCG report on financial statement restatements was retrieved using the key words "financial statement restatements" through the Google search engine of America Online. This search resulted in several related websites, each of which was examined. Two of these were the websites, www.iasplus.com/resource/huron2003 and http://www.huronconsultinggroup.com/uploadedFiles/Huron_2004_Review%20of%20Fi nancial%20Reporting%20Matters.pdf. The first website contained the *2003 Annual Review of Financial Reporting Matters,* and the second website contained the *2004 Annual Review of Financial Reporting Matters: Final Report* from the HCG, with the designated statistics concerning restatements by year filed, audited 10K and 10Q restatements, and restated annual financial statements.

The SEC website also produced the Reports on Administrative Proceedings from which data was gathered. On the website home page located at www.sec.gov, the key words rulings, litigation, and proceedings were typed into the website search field. The word proceedings produced the reports at www.sec.gov/news/studies/, with each six month report at its own extension of this main web address. The reports for October 1, 1996 through March 31, 2005 were located using this method.

The data selected is appropriate for the study in that it provides some different aspects of the reaction of the SEC to the provisions of SOX, through the display of the litigation numbers, from the CFTF reports, and by use of the statistics from the Reports on Administrative Proceedings. The report on financial statement restatements by the HCG demonstrates the reaction of corporations to the enactment of the SOX litigation. The analysis of any difference between the data prior to and subsequent to SOX will demonstrate if a rejoinder to the law is in effect and if it is substantial enough to be noteworthy.

Selection and Description of Data

The four types of reported data utilized in the analysis were selected because of their perceived representations of statistics that would be affected by the enactment of SOX. These numbers were also chosen due to the ability of the data to be quantitatively analyzed.

The first data group is entitled SEC enforcement statistics, and involves types of SEC actions against public corporations by the Division of Enforcement, which "investigates possible violations of securities laws, recommends Commission action when appropriate, either in a federal court or before an administrative law judge, and negotiates settlements" (SEC, 2004/2, p. 1). See Appendix B for the five categories of statistics utilized in the analysis.

The second data group is data from the CFTF first and second year reports to the President. The CFTF originated with the enactment of Executive Order 13271 on July 9, 2002, and is comprised of 18 highly respected individuals from several United States agencies, including the Department of Justice, the Federal Bureau of Investigation, the Department of Labor, the Postal Inspection Service, and the SEC. The main tasks of the CFTF are to "provide direction for the investigation and prosecution of cases of securities fraud, accounting fraud" (CFTF, 2003, p. 1.2) as well as other types of fraud, and to provide recommendations to the Attorney General and the President in regard to resource allocations and the enforcement of financial crimes (CFTF, 2003, p. 1.2). The reports of the CFTF are designed to demonstrate the progress of the CFTF through the use of narrative and statistics, including the statistics of the financial crime enforcement actions of the SEC. See Appendix C for the SEC statistics presented in the reports and analyzed in this study.

Financial statement restatements data comprise the third data group, as reported by the HCG in which it "examines the actions taken by the U.S. Securities and Exchange Commission (SEC), the Public Company Accounting Oversight Board (PCAOB) and the Financial Accounting Standards Board (FASB)" (Huron Consulting Group, 2004, p. 2). The purpose of the examination was to "gather data on the size and industry of the registrants that experienced a restatement problem, and, ultimately, to review the underlying accounting error that necessitated the restatement" (Huron Consulting Group, 2004, p. 2). The statistics in Appendix D demonstrate the number and type of financial statement restatements discovered by the HCG before and after the enactment of SOX.

The fourth data set is from the SEC Reports on Administrative Proceedings, which are required to be issued semi-annually by the SEC secretary in order to comply with Rule 900 of the Commission's Rules of Practice. These reports identify "the number of matters pending before the administrative law judges and the Commission at the beginning of the six-month period; the number of matters instituted, filed, and disposed of during the period; and the number pending at the end of the period" (SEC, 2004/1, p. 1). The new matters added during the period comprise the data selected for the analysis (see Appendix E).

Instrumentation

Unpaired T Test

The unpaired t test was chosen as one type of instrumentation appropriate in the analysis of the relationship between the two groups of numbers prior to and subsequent to the passage of SOX because certain assumptions were met. The independence assumption is fulfilled because the two groups of numbers being analyzed span different time periods and a "systematic relationship between observations" (Virginia University, 2003, p. 1) does not exist. Also, most of the pre-SOX data groups and the post-SOX data groups with which they were compared have similar variances, as measured by the test of equality of variances. This satisfies another t test assumption. In addition, the t test assumes that the dependent variable groups have a normal distribution. In the data sets examined in this study, some of the sets were small in number, and normal distribution in small data sets is difficult to determine because "small samples simply don't contain enough information to let you make inferences about the shape of the distribution in the entire population" (Prism, 2004, pp. 3-4). However, "both assumptions [homogeneity of variance and normal distribution] can be violated without much effect to our study results. The homogeneity of variance assumption is typically regarded as the more important assumption" (Kisamore, 2003, p. 1). Since two of the important assumptions of the t test were met, the t test was one tool utilized to analyze the data collected.

The next task was to determine if a paired or unpaired t test should be run for the group comparisons. The paired t test is utilized when "two columns of data are matched" (Prism, 2004, p. 1), or when "subjects are matched in pairs and each treatment is given to one subject in each pair randomly" (Hahn, 2003, p. 1). Also, the paired t test is used for comparisons in which "the measures were taken on the same individuals on two different occasions, or that there is some other inherent dependency among the groups" (Kam, 2002, p. 2). In the data sets examined in this study, no dependency exists among the groups compared, nor are the groups matched because of similarity of certain characteristics. The differences of the means of the groups in each category were analyzed based on their proximity to the enactment of SOX, and in all cases the numbers in the pre-SOX data sets do not correlate to the numbers in the post-SOX data sets. The determination was thus made to use the unpaired t test to analyze the data. Because both hypotheses were concerned with the negative as well as the positive impact of SOX, the two-tailed unpaired t test was utilized.

Chi Square Test

The decision was made to employ another statistical test in order to further compare the two sets of data, and to also determine if this test would support the findings of the other test. A non-parametric test of statistical significance, the chi square test, was chosen for the analysis. This test is appropriate to compare the data sets because it assists in the determination of whether the two statistical groups "are different enough in some characteristic or aspect of their behavior that we can generalize from our samples that the populations from which our samples are drawn are also different" (Connor-Linton, 2003, p.1). Chi square accomplishes this by comparing "what actually happened to what hypothetically would have happened if 'all other things were equal' (basically, the null hypothesis)" (Connor-Linton, p.6).

Chi square analyzes the data in bivariate tables. For this analysis to be effective, certain requirements should be met. These requirements include (a) the samples should be randomly taken from the population, (b) the data must not be reported in percentages, (c) the variables that are used must be independent, (d) the values of the independent and dependent variables should be exclusive, and (e) the frequencies observed cannot be too small (Connor-Linton, 2003). The data utilized for the analysis for this study do meet these requirements. The statistics used were randomly selected from enforcement and other statistics available related to possible reactionary procedures imposed subsequent to the passage of SOX. Also, the data is reported in actual numbers, and the independent variable which exists for the study is exclusive of the dependent variables. Two sets of data within the data analyzed, trading suspensions within the SEC enforcement data and interlocutory motions within the SEC Reports on Administrative Proceedings data, contain zero and near-zero frequencies, for which chi square cannot calculate a reliable conclusion (Connor-Linton, 2003). Therefore, these two sets of data were not analyzed using the chi square methodology. However, performing the chi square analysis on the remainder of the data was determined to be sufficiently valuable.

Validity and Reliability

In researching the data available in order to evaluate the effectiveness of SOX, many studies, reports, and surveys were examined along with the four sets of data selected for investigation. Among these were the testimony of SEC chairman William H. Donaldson on the implementation of SOX; the study by the international economic consulting firm, NERA, on the impact of SOX on securities class actions filed, encompassing the years from 1991 to 2003; the Parson Consulting survey on SOX compliance; the Robert Half survey on privately held companies in compliance with SOX; the Association of Certified Fraud Examiners (ACFE) Reports to the Nation for 2002 as well as for 2004; the study of SEC enforcement actions over five years, as mandated by Section 704 of SOX for the period between July, 1997 and July 2002; SEC Protecting Investors Annual Reports for 2002 and 2003; and other sources. The data selected for analysis were considered to be the most representational of the actions occurring prior to and subsequent to SOX, as well as being the most measurable with the statistical instrumentation available.

In addition, different statistical methods were examined with which to evaluate the selected data. Meta analysis was considered, but was rejected because it is a method by which to analyze several studies concerning the same type of data, which would not have provided the appropriate results for this study. A test of means was determined to be the best method available to compare the data between the two time periods. A nonparametric test of means, the Mann-Whitney U test, was considered. However, this test was also rejected because the two important assumptions were met for the parametric t test, which is considered preferable because "nonparametric tests have less 'power' to detect a significant difference" (Jones, 2004, p. 5) while "parametric procedures are relatively robust to departures" (Osenberg, 2003, p. 4) from basic assumptions. The analysis of variance test was examined as well, but the results of this type of test with two sets of data would be identical to the results of the t test. Therefore, the two-tailed unpaired t test was selected as one of the tests suitable for the analysis of the four categories of data sets.

Another test, the non-parametric chi square test, was also chosen to examine the statistics. The chi square test assesses the significance level of difference between the two sets of data, and even though the method is a less powerful non-parametric test, the use of chi square was valuable in providing more analysis of the numerical information. In addition, the test produced data that could be compared with the unpaired t test results. In essence, the chi square analysis assisted with the objective of both tests, which is to prove or disprove the null hypothesis.

Data Processing and Analysis

Each category of data was separated into pre-SOX and post-SOX groups. The SEC enforcement numbers are monthly data. The statistics from the CFTF first and second year reports to the President and the HCG financial statement restatements represent one year results, while the data sets from the SEC Reports on Administrative Proceedings each span six months. Because SOX was passed into law on July 30, 2002, the data had to be split between prior to and including July of 2002, and subsequent to and including August of 2002.

Unpaired T Test

The SEC enforcement statistics are made up of individual suits and actions reported by the SEC. The reported data as retrieved were manually counted to result in monthly figures. These monthly figures were easily divided into pre-SOX and post-SOX values for the unpaired t test analysis by dividing them between July, 2002 and August, 2002.

The data from the CFTF first and second year reports to the President were presented in annual form, according to the SEC fiscal year. In order to divide this data for the SEC fiscal year from October of 2001 to September of 2002 into pre-SOX and post-SOX data for the unpaired t test, a formula had to be devised for this 12 month increment. The monthly data from the SEC enforcement statistics was used for these formulas (see Appendix B). The data for the months from October, 2001 to September, 2002 of the SEC enforcement statistics were added to get an annual result in each of the five categories. The figures for August, 2002 and September, 2002 were summed, and then divided by the annual result. This produced five percentages. The highest percentage and the lowest percentage were discarded so as not to skew the information. The resulting three percentages were divided by three to result in the rate of 16.04% to be used for August and September of 2002. But because in this case the data had to represent twelve months to be comparable to the rest of the data, the October of 2001 through September of 2002 numbers for the CFTF data were multiplied by 16.04% to represent the August and September figures, divided by two to result in one month figures, which were then multiplied by twelve to result in the comparable post-SOX annual figures. In order to extract the October through July figure, the October of 2001

75

through September of 2002 numbers were multiplied by 83.96% (100%-16.04%), which were then divided by ten and also multiplied by twelve to result in the annual pre-SOX figures. Again for the sake of comparability, this actually resulted in two twelve month figures for the time period of October, 2001 through September of 2002 (see Appendix C).

The HCG financial statement restatement data was presented annually as well, but using calendar year data. Once again, the SEC enforcement statistics were utilized in order to separate the pre-SOX and post-SOX numbers for analysis for the calendar year from January of 2002 to December of 2002 (see Appendix B). The corresponding SEC enforcement statistics for these months were added to get an annual result in each of the five categories. The data for August, 2002 through December, 2002 were added, and then divided by the annual result. This once more produced five percentages. Again, the highest percentage and the lowest percentage were discarded so as not to skew the figures. The resulting three percentages were divided by three to result in the rate of 40.29% to be used for August through December of 2002. As previously, the data had to represent twelve months to be comparable to the rest of the data. Therefore, the calendar year 2002 numbers for the financial statement restatement data were multiplied by 40.29% to represent the August through December figures, divided by five to result in one month figures, which were then multiplied by twelve to result in the comparable post-SOX annual figures. In order to extract the January through July figure, the calendar year 2002 numbers were multiplied by 59.71% (100%-40.29%), which were then divided by seven and multiplied by twelve to result in the annual pre-SOX figures. This calculation again actually resulted in two twelve month figures for the time period of

January, 2002 through December, 2002, but was necessary for proper comparisons (see Appendix D).

The data from the SEC Reports on Administrative Proceedings was grouped in six month intervals, based on the SEC fiscal year, which operates from October to September. One six month increment encompassed the months from October to March, and the second six month increment for that same year encompassed the months from April to September. In order to divide the data for the unpaired t test for the SEC fiscal year from October of 2001 to September of 2002 into pre-SOX and post-SOX data, another formula had to be devised for each of the six month increments from April of 2002 to September of 2002. Again, the data from the SEC enforcement statistics was used for these formulas (see Appendix B). The data for the months from April, 2002 to September, 2002 of the SEC enforcement statistics were summed to get a six month result in each of the five categories. The data for August, 2002 and September, 2002 were added, and then divided by the six month result. Once more, this produced five percentages. The highest percentage and the lowest percentage were again discarded so as not to skew the numbers. The resulting three percentages were divided by three to result in the rate of 30.47% to be used for August and September of 2002. But because the data had to represent six months to be comparable to the rest of the data, the April through September of 2002 numbers for the administrative proceedings data were multiplied by 30.47% to represent the August and September figures, divided by two to result in one month figures, which were then multiplied by six to result in the comparable post-SOX six month figures. In order to extract the April through July figure, the April through September of 2002 numbers were multiplied by 69.53% (100%-30.47%), which were then divided by four and multiplied by six to result in the six month pre-SOX figures. This actually resulted in two six month figures for the time period of April through September of 2002, but this was necessary in order to result in equivalent statistical information (see Appendix E).

As noted previously, the unpaired t test was one method utilized to analyze the data. In the t test, the t value is calculated using the formula

$$t = \frac{X1 - X2}{Sx1\text{-}x2}$$

where X1 is the mean of the pre-SOX group and X2 is the mean of the post-SOX group. The standard error of the difference between the means is calculated by the formula Sx1-x2. A two-tailed unpaired t test was used in each of the calculations, with the level of significance at 0.05.

Chi Square Test

As mentioned earlier, the chi square test employs a bivariate table. This table cannot contain zero or near-zero values (Connor-Linton, 2003) and must include the same number of values in each row of the table. The CFTF categories follow these requirements, so no manipulation of the data was necessary. However, the post-SOX and pre-SOX number of values reported in the financial statement restatements are not equal. So only the two most recent pre-SOX figures were analyzed in order to equalize the table. The same issue occurred with the SEC Reports on Administrative Proceedings sets of statistics. Only the six most recent pre-SOX figures were used in the chi square comparison of the data. However, as discussed in the instrumentation section, the interlocutory motions category could not be analyzed using the chi square test because it contains zero and near-zero values.

The SEC enforcement statistics required additional massaging. Not only are the number of pre-SOX and post-SOX figures different, but the amount of numbers of each resulted in degrees of freedom that were too large to provide for an effective chi square analysis. Therefore, four consecutive months were combined for both the pre-SOX and post-SOX data, causing nine of the oldest post-SOX numbers and two of the oldest pre-SOX numbers to remain unused. The most recent post-SOX figures were selected for analysis in order to evaluate the most current statistics available as SOX is evolving. The most recent pre-SOX figures were also used because it was felt that they would be more comparable to the post-SOX statistics. These groupings of the pre-SOX and post-SOX statistics resulted in a two by eight bivariate table, which was available for analysis using the chi square test. But as previously revealed, the trading suspensions category could not be analyzed using this method because it contains zero numbers.

The chi square value is calculated using the formula

$$X^2 = \Sigma n \,[(Po-Pe)^2/Pe]$$

where X^2 is the chi square statistic, Σ is the sum of, n is the number of total observations in each column, Po is the proportion of observed frequencies in each cell, and Pe is the expected proportion for each row. The degrees of freedom is calculated with the formula (r-1)(c-1), where r is the number of rows in the bivariate table, and c is the number of columns in the table (McMillan & Schumacher, 2001).

Methodological Assumptions

An assumption is not an assertion, but a statement to be tested for accuracy (Kaplan, 1998). The main methodological assumption used in the study is that the unpaired t test and the chi square test are the best methods of testing the means of the pre-

SOX and post-SOX groups. Along with this, the assumption has also been made that the unpaired t test and the chi square test are appropriate to analyze the data sets composed of only a few numbers. This by all appearances would seem to be the case based on the expectation of the outcome of the analyses and the overall general comparison of the groups of numbers without applying the unpaired t test and chi square instruments.

Another assumption made is that the mathematical formulas utilized in dividing the six-month and annual data into pre-SOX (July, 2002 and prior) and post-SOX (August, 2002 and subsequent) numbers are suitable. However, due to the similarities of the data in most of the groups during the months before and after the passage of SOX, evenly dividing the six-month or annual numbers between each of the months would probably have led to virtually the same outcomes.

An additional assumption made similar to the previous one is that the use of just the most recent pre-SOX numbers while also eliminating some of the earliest post-SOX numbers for the SEC enforcement statistics categories, in order to create even chi square bivariate tables, is a proper procedure. It is assumed that this abbreviated use of the pre-SOX and post-SOX data is indicative of enforcement and restatement developments occurring prior to and subsequent to the passage of SOX, and that the corresponding results of the chi square test are valid and reliable.

Other assumptions have been made. One is that the data used in the analysis is representative of the trends of SOX and signifies its effectiveness on the prevention and detection of fraud in financial statements. Another assumption is that the figures actually represent the events that comprise the general reactions prior to and subsequent to the passage of SOX. Also, the assumption has been made that statistical data is the most useful in the analysis, leading to appropriate conclusions. Because SOX is only approximately three years old, these assumptions can only be determined to be accurate after the passage of time and further examination by various sources.

Limitations

The most striking limitation in this study is that due to the recent passage of SOX in July of 2002, data is available for only the two to three years subsequent to its passage into law. The distinct possibility exists that as the years progress, SOX may be proven to be more effective or less effective in fraud prevention and detection than the results of this study would indicate. But only time can bear witness to whichever outcome will emerge.

Also, some bias may be demonstrated in the interpretation of the outcome of the data analysis. Bias can be defined as "tending to yield an outcome more frequently than others in a statistical experiment", or as "a highly personal and unreasoned distortion of judgment (prejudice)" (Oklahoma State University, 2004, p. 1). For instance, a corporate CFO who is unhappy with the restrictions and provisions of SOX would have a tendency to interpret the data to result in the ineffectiveness of SOX, while Senator Sarbanes or Congressman Oxley, the Congressmen who are credited with the authorship of the legislation, would tend to interpret the data in a much more favorable light. In order to combat the problem of bias, the interpreter of the data should be aware of any preconceived tendencies, and analyze the information as objectively as possible. Other such leanings could have been present when the raw data was gathered by the different reporting entities. This would be very difficult to expose, but must be a consideration in the examination of the figures. However, on the positive side, quantitative data by its nature is less available for interpretation, which provides for better objectivity and less bias than a more qualitative approach.

Conceptual Hypotheses

In this study, the conceptual hypotheses are similar to the statistical hypotheses which were the focus in this chapter. For the research question of whether SOX is effective, the null hypothesis would be that SOX is not effective in preventing and detecting fraud. The alternative hypothesis would be that SOX is effective in preventing and detecting fraud. A Type I error would occur if the research led to the conclusion that SOX is effective, when it is not. A Type II error would occur if the research led to the conclusion that SOX is not effective when in fact it is.

The purpose of the data analysis instruments utilized in this chapter are to support the null hypothesis or support the alternative hypothesis. From the results, the possibility of Type I or Type II errors can be examined in order to determine the reliability of the conclusions drawn from the analysis.

Summary of Methodology and Procedures

In order to ascertain the effectiveness of SOX in preventing and detecting fraud in financial statements, four groups of statistics were gathered from reports by reputable sources. Each data set within each group was divided into pre-SOX and post-SOX numbers, and a test of means and a test of statistical significance were applied to each divided data set. The unpaired two-tailed t test was used to test the means to provide support for the null hypothesis, which states that the passage of SOX causes no difference, either positively or negatively, as to the prevention and detection of fraud, or for the alternative hypothesis, which states that SOX does make a difference, whether positively or negatively, in the prevention and detection of fraud in financial statements. The chi square test was utilized to test for significant differences between the pre-SOX and post-SOX data, again to sustain either the null hypothesis or the alternative hypothesis.

In Chapter Four, the results of the data analysis will be examined and interpreted as to their support of the null hypothesis or the alternative hypothesis. Chapter Four will also introduce an eight question survey (see Appendix H) that was emailed to various accounting firms and corporations to add a more human element in the analysis of the success of SOX in achieving its intended purposes.

CHAPTER FOUR: RESULTS AND FINDINGS

In Chapter Three, the data groups to be examined in the procedural statistical analysis as related to the research questions concerning SOX were introduced and discussed. The four data groups exhaustively detailed were SEC enforcement statistics, data from the CFTF first and second year reports to the President, financial statement restatements as reported by HCG, and statistics from the SEC Reports on Administrative Proceedings. Also established in Chapter Three were the two methods of statistical analysis to be used to scrutinize the data, namely the unpaired t test and the chi square test. A survey was mentioned as well to be distributed and evaluated with the intentions of determining the human response to SOX and the consequences of the legislation.

In this chapter, the statistical analysis methods will be executed, and the corresponding results will then be assessed as to their responsiveness to the research questions. The survey replies will also be discussed and deciphered as well, again in correlation to the validity of the research questions and the conclusions drawn from the survey response.

These research questions were detailed in Chapters One and Three. Briefly, the main one echoes the title of this study, namely whether or not SOX is effective in the prevention and detection of fraud in financial statements. And if not, should the legislation be revised, or simply eliminated altogether. Other research questions include whether the cost of SOX to corporations is worth the benefits, as well as determining if investor confidence in the securities market has been improved by the passage of SOX.

Description of Data Collection

Unpaired T Test and Chi Square Test

The data for the unpaired t test and the chi square test, the two statistical analysis methods used in the study, were collected simply by running the two types of tests on each category within the four data groups. The categories available totaled 20, each of which was examined using the unpaired t test method. Two categories were not analyzed using the chi square test due to the existence of zero values within the data, which cannot be processed by this analysis method. The other categories were successfully inspected using the chi square test.

Each test for each category was run at least two times to ensure the accurate input of data and the resulting output. For the unpaired t test, the pre-SOX data were entered into the first column, while the post-SOX data were entered into the second column. For 15 of the 20 categories, this resulted in a negative mean difference as well as a negative t value. For the chi square test, both the pre-SOX and post-SOX statistics were listed in the order of most recent to oldest. The placement of the pre-SOX data and the post-SOX data into different rows and columns was tested, with no difference in the outcome of the test. The presented tests were conducted placing the post-SOX figures in the first row and the pre-SOX figures in the second row.

Survey

The data collection for the survey method of analysis for the study involved emailing surveys over the Internet, as well as some telephone interviews. Around 500 surveys were emailed, with the result of 52 completed and returned. One respondent chose to enclose comments on SOX in the email rather than to answer the survey questions specifically. Two of those surveyed requested additional communication in order to enhance their written comments, so telephone contact was made to further discuss the issues of SOX.

The data were then gathered onto one survey sheet, shown in Appendix I, for comparison purposes. By this method, general trends could be distinguished according to type of respondent and to type of company by which they were employed. Any separate comments made on the surveys and by phone conversation have also been recorded on the survey sheet in Appendix I.

Demographic Data

The surveys required use of demographics from which to draw the random sample of prospective respondents selected to receive the questions. The most relevant recipients on the topic of the effectiveness of SOX in the prevention and detection of fraud in financial statements were determined to be certified public accountants working in the arena of public accounting, and chief financial officers and other management personnel in public as well as some private companies who would be encountering the regulations of SOX on a daily basis.

Both groups were developed using the Internet. Accountants in CPA firms were found by typing "CPA firms" into the America Online search engine. The website, cpafirms.com, was discovered using this process, and it contains CPA firms from every state in the U.S. The website of the National Association of Certified Public Accounting Firms also appeared during this search, with the web address of nacpa.com. Approximately 50 firms from both of these websites were randomly selected to receive the survey. Six surveys were returned from this group. The independent auditor for the non-profit agency by which the author of the study is employed was also requested to complete a survey, which was filled out and returned. One continuing professional education instructor, who is also a CPA and who conducted a class previously completed by the author, also complied with responses to the survey. One CPA requested further discussion through a telephone conversation, which was done.

Several lists of CFOs and other executives from around the country were acquired through the website lead411.com. Approximately 450 companies were randomly selected from these lists to receive the surveys, which were mostly sent to CFOs. However, some were also emailed to CEOs, chief operating officers (COOs), vice presidents (VPs), and a few in other management positions. One CFO of a major international brewing company also requested a telephone conversation for clarification of comments as well as a dialogue concerning the current survey results and additional views.

Results

Unpaired T Test

The printouts of the outcomes of the unpaired t tests applied to the twenty categories are contained in Appendix F. The results of the unpaired t tests are displayed in Table 1 for each of the categories.

Table 1			
T Test Results			
Reports	t score	p value	Degree of Difference
SEC Enforcement Statistics			
Federal Court Actions	-2.70	0.009	Very Statistically Significant Difference

Admininstrative Law Judges Initial Decisions & Orders	-2.51	0.014	Statistically Significant Difference
Administrative Proceedings	-4.34	<= 0.001	Extremely Statistically Significant Difference
Commission Opinions	-3.47	<= 0.001	Very Statistically Significant Difference
Trading Suspensions	-2.22	0.03	Statistically Significant Difference
CFTF Reports			
Total SEC Enforcement Actions Filed	-0.90	0.42	No Statistically Significant Difference
Financial Fraud and Issuer Reporting Actions Filed	-0.87	0.43	No Statistically Significant Difference
Officer and Director Bars Sought	-2.45	0.07	Not Quite Statistically Significant Difference
Temporary Restraining Orders Filed	-0.25	0.82	No Statistically Significant Difference
Asset Freezes	0.57	0.60	No Statistically Significant Difference
Subpoena Enforcement Proceedings	0.22	0.83	No Statistically Significant Difference
Financial Statement Restatements			
Restatements by Year Filed	-2.13	0.09	Not Quite Statistically Significant Difference
Audited 10K Restatements by Year Filed	-2.60	0.05	Statistically Significant Difference

Audited 10Q Restatements by Year Filed	-0.68	0.53	No Statistically Significant Difference
Restated Annual Financial Statements	-2.76	0.04	Statistically Significant Difference
SEC Reports on Administrative Proceedings			
Matters Before the Administrative Law Judges	-1.67	0.12	No Statistically Significant Difference
Matters Before the Commission	0.58	0.57	No Statistically Significant Difference
Review of Self-Regulatory Organization Decisions	1.20	0.25	No Statistically Significant Difference
Interlocutory Motions	0.72	0.48	No Statistically Significant Difference
Stay Requests	-0.01	0.99	No Statistically Significant Difference

Note: 0.05% level of significance used in all tests.

Of the 20 categories examined using the unpaired t test, administrative proceedings reported within the SEC enforcement statistics group contains an extremely statistically different result between pre-SOX data and post-SOX data. Appendix F contains the means for the two types of figures in this category. The mean of the pre-SOX data for the administrative proceedings is 28.06 and 40.29 for the post-SOX mean. This set of means indicates that the post-SOX figures, on average, contain larger values.

A very statistically significant difference between the pre-SOX and the post-SOX numbers is shown in two of the 20 categories. These two categories are both within the SEC enforcement statistics group as well, and they are federal court actions and commission opinions. Again, the means displayed for both categories in Appendix F

demonstrate that the post-SOX data are larger, on average, than the pre-SOX data.

A statistically significant difference between the pre-SOX and the post-SOX data

appeared in four of the categories. Two categories, administrative law judges initial

decisions and orders, and trade suspensions, are contained within the SEC enforcement

statistics group. The other two categories, audited 10K restatements by year filed and

restated annual financial statements, are within the financial statement restatements

group. Once again all the post-SOX means of all four categories are larger than the pre-

SOX means.

The other 13 categories tested utilizing the unpaired t test resulted in 11

demonstrating no statistically significant difference between pre-SOX and post-SOX

data, and two indicating a not quite statistically significant difference. Both of these

results signify that not enough disparity is evident between the values in order for the

unpaired t test to conclude that a numerical differentiation exists.

Chi Square Test

The printouts of the effects of the chi square test applied to the 18 categories are

displayed in Appendix G. Table 2 summarizes the results of these tests. As mentioned

previously, two of the categories contain zero values, and thus could not be analyzed by

the chi square test.

Table 2			
Chi Square Test Results			
Reports	chi square	p value	Degree of Difference

SEC Enforcement Statistics

Federal Court Actions	43.61	<= 0.001	Distribution is Significant
Admininstrative Law Judges Initial Decisions & Orders	5.62	<= 1.00	Distribution Not Significant
Administrative Proceedings	29.38	<= 0.001	Distribution is Significant
Commission Opinions	18.13	<= 0.025	Distribution is Significant
Trading Suspensions	N/A - Contains Zero Values		

CFTF Reports

Total SEC Enforcement Actions Filed	37.90	<= 0.001	Distribution is Significant
Financial Fraud and Issuer Reporting Actions Filed	39.00	<= 0.001	Distribution is Significant
Officer and Director Bars Sought	28.31	<= 0.001	Distribution is Significant
Temporary Restraining Orders Filed	4.15	<= 0.20	Distribution Not Significant
Asset Freezes	1.83	<= 1.00	Distribution Not Significant
Subpoena Enforcement Proceedings	7.93	<= 0.025	Distribution is Significant

Financial Statement Restatements

Restatements by Year Filed	1.47	<= 1.00	Distribution

			Not Significant
Audited 10K Restatements by Year Filed	3.38	<= 0.20	Distribution Not Significant
Audited 10Q Restatements by Year Filed	1.20	<= 1.00	Distribution Not Significant
Restated Annual Financial Statements	2.16	<= 1.00	Distribution Not Significant
SEC Reports on Administrative Proceedings			
Matters Before the Administrative Law Judges	22.82	<= 0.001	Distribution is Significant
Matters Before the Commission	3.41	<= 1.00	Distribution Not Significant
Review of Self-Regulatory Organization Decisions	7.10	<= 1.00	Distribution Not Significant
Interlocutory Motions	N/A - Contains Zero Values		
Stay Requests	4.90	<= 1.00	Distribution Not Significant

Note: 0.05% level of significance used in all tests.

Of the 18 categories that were able to be tested, eight sets of data were disparate enough to cause a significant distribution result between post-SOX and pre-SOX values. These categories include (a) three in the SEC enforcement statistics group, federal court actions, administrative proceedings, and commission opinions, all also containing a statistical difference result by means of the unpaired t test; (b) total SEC enforcement actions filed, financial fraud and issuer reporting actions filed, officer and director bars sought, and subpoena enforcement proceedings, all in the CFTF reports group; and (c) matters before the administrative law judges in the SEC reports on administrative proceedings group.

As mentioned in Chapter Three, for two of the groups, which are the financial statement restatements group and the SEC reports on administrative proceedings group, some of the earliest pre-SOX values obtained could not be used in order to ensure that each chi square grid had an equivalent number of columns. For the SEC enforcement statistics group, the values had to be grouped into four-month totals, while two of the earliest pre-SOX values and nine of the earliest post-SOX values could also not be used, to allow the data to be able to fit into an even chi square grid. Despite these adjustments, most of the means of the two types of pre-SOX data were relatively similar, whether all values were used or the adjusted number of values was used. The unadjusted and adjusted post-SOX means for the SEC enforcement statistics group are also quite similar.

However, for the matters before the administrative law judges category, the mean of the chi square pre-SOX adjusted number of values is 21.56, while the unpaired t test pre-SOX mean is 29.53. The post-SOX mean is 42.06. The larger difference between the post-SOX value and the pre-SOX value for the chi square test clarifies why a statistical difference exists using the chi square test, while no statistical difference is apparent utilizing the unpaired t test.

Conversely, for the audited 10K restatements by year filed and the restated annual financial statements, the unpaired t test found a statistically significant difference between pre-SOX and post-SOX data, while the chi square test found none. This could be due to the larger means of the pre-SOX data in the chi square values, causing the means to be closer in value to the post-SOX means, resulting in no significant difference for the chi square tests.

Another category, subpoena enforcement proceedings, with a p value of <=0.025, is indicating a statistical difference by a slender margin. The means of the post-SOX and pre-SOX data are very close in value, displaying a post-SOX value of 13.09 and a slightly larger pre-SOX value of 14.05. The other five categories demonstrating statistical differences by the chi square test are exhibiting larger post-SOX means than pre-SOX means.

The other 10 categories analyzed using the chi square test resulted in the distribution between the two sets of data being not significant. This indicates that no statistical difference is evident between the post-SOX and pre-SOX data in these categories.

Survey

The results of the survey responses are not as easy to quantify, but provide for interesting insight as well as fascinating perusal of the comments. Appendix I contains the specific survey results separated by job classification of the respondents, as well as by the type of company by which the executive respondents are employed, either public or private. Most of the comments provided by the respondents are also included in Appendix I. In total, 52 completed surveys were collected.

CPAs that responded to the survey numbered eight. Of the executives that replied, 28 were CFOs and chief accounting officers (CAOs). The number of COOs was two, while the number of CEOs was also two. The number of VPs was six, and six respondents fell into the other category.

The surveys were returned by 44 people in executive positions, with 29 employed by public companies and 15 employed by privately held companies. Of the public companies represented by respondents, the stocks of 16 companies were traded on the National Association of Securities Dealers Automated Quotations (NASDAQ) market, nine traded on the NYSE, two on the American Stock Exchange (AMEX), one on the Over the Counter Bulletin Board (OTC) market, and one quoted on the pink sheet system.

The detailed responses by job classification and company type can be found in Appendix I, but a very summarized version is displayed in Table 3.

Table 3 Summarized Survey Results			
Question	Strongly Agree or Agree	No Opinion	Strongly Disagree or Disagree
1	50	0	2
2	45	0	7
3	20	0	2
4	52	0	0
5	6	5	41
6	18	9	25
7	46	4	2
8	13	1	38

Question One addressed the issue of whether SOX has changed the way accountants perform audits, and two CPAs provided the only dissenting opinions.

Question Two asked whether SOX has also changed the way companies perform their accounting tasks and the majority agreed or strongly agreed. Question Three was inadvertently omitted from many of the surveys that were sent, but of the 22 executives that responded to this question, all but two strongly agreed or agreed that the attitude of company management toward the audit has changed due to SOX. The inquiry in Question Four of whether more work-related opportunities for accountants have arisen because of the passage of SOX resulted in the strongly agreed or agreed reaction by all respondents. On the pertinent issue of whether or not the benefits of SOX are worth the cost in Question Five, 41 disagreed or strongly disagreed. However, six did agree while five had no opinion.

The Question Six inquiry as to the effectiveness of SOX in the prevention and detection of fraud in financial statements resulted in differing responses, with 25 of the total 52 replying in the negative, while nine had no opinion. The majority of respondents of all classifications strongly agreed or agreed that SOX should be modified, per Question Seven. But Question Eight, which asked whether SOX should be eliminated, elicited 30 disagree responses and eight strongly disagree responses, with 13 believing that the legislation should be eliminated entirely.

Non-Predicted Non-Significant Findings Discussion

Though the general results of the unpaired t test, the chi square test, and the survey are not surprising, some interesting events occurred during the survey data collection. Of the 28 CFOs and CAOs that responded to the survey, 17 of them did not wish their names or the names of their companies mentioned in the study. Of the CFOs and CAOs that consented to the mentioning of their names, eight were from public companies and three were from private companies. All of the CPAs agreed to the mentioning of names and firms, while nine of the 16 other executives wished to remain anonymous, all of them from public companies.

Of the numerous surveys that were emailed out, it was discovered that only 8.9% of the targeted executives that were subsequently emailed were women, while only 12.7% of the available CPAs that were selected for emailing were women. Of the respondents, only 11.4% of the executives were women and only 12.5% of the CPAs were women.

A couple of the respondents, a CPA as well as a CFO of a national brewing company, wished to be contacted by telephone to discuss their viewpoints further. Another CFO had a great deal to share concerning SOX, and included a two page discussion with the survey response. An executive that fell into the other category also included extended remarks with the survey. The implications are that SOX is a relevant topic, sometimes eliciting strong opinions and reactions.

Interpretation

Unpaired T Test and Chi Square Test

The results of the unpaired t test reveal that seven of the 20 tests run on the different categories present some kind of a significant difference between pre-SOX data and post-SOX data. Of those seven, one resulted in an extremely statistically significant difference, two revealed a very statistically significant difference, while four produced only a statistically significant difference.

The chi square test divulged a slightly different result. Of the 18 tests performed on the executable data, eight display a significant difference in the distribution of the data. However, in one of these eight, the subpoena enforcement proceedings from the CFTF reports, the mean of the pre-SOX data is greater than the mean of the post-SOX data. This leads to the inference that in only seven of these eight differences has SOX caused more enforcements actions and procedures than occurred prior to SOX.

The results of the unpaired t test conclude that in 13 of 20, or 65%, of the statistical analyses completed, no difference exists between pre-SOX data and post-SOX data. As well, the chi square test results provide that 11 of 18, or 61%, of the tests conclude that no significant difference is evident between the data, or that in the one instance, pre-SOX figures are actually greater than post-SOX figures. Both of these testing procedures, though not overwhelming in their conclusions, lead to the deduction that the difference between pre-SOX data and post-SOX data is minimal. Thus both of these tests, as executed on the data selected, direct the reader to the conclusion that the null hypothesis is correct, namely that SOX, in the majority of cases, is not effective in the prevention and detection of fraud in financial statements. This is, of course, provided that previous suppositions are correct.

These results are contingent upon several factors. The appropriateness of the selection of the data addresses threats to both internal and external validity. It is possible that different conclusions would be displayed if different types and categories of data had been selected. The statistical conclusions from the testing are also a threat to internal validity, possibly because some of the data sets are small, and also possibly because the assumptions used to analyze the data may be inappropriate, one of which is the assumption that the data groups selected are representative of enforcements and proceedings associated with SOX. Time measurement is a threat to external validity, due to the fact that only two to three years of post-SOX data are currently available. Future statistics developed over a number of years subsequent to the enactment of SOX may provide for a different outcome, given the same instrumentation.

Had the statistical analysis decidedly demonstrated that the occurrences of enforcement actions and restatements were greater subsequent to SOX as opposed to prior to SOX, then the argument could be developed that SOX was providing for better detection of fraud, but not better prevention. Conversely, if the statistical analysis had resulted in the pre-SOX data demonstrating more enforcement actions and restatements than post-SOX data, the discussion would ensue that SOX is possibly creating better prevention of fraud than prior to its enactment. But the statistical analysis demonstrates that in the majority of cases, very little difference between the pre-SOX data and the post-SOX data is evident, resulting in the conclusion that SOX makes no difference in the prevention and detection of fraud in financial statements.

Survey

According to the results of the survey, the majority of all categories agree that SOX has created changes in the way accountants perform audits and in the way companies perform their accounting tasks. However, the majority responding agree that the attitude of company management toward the audit has also changed. All agree that the work-related opportunities for accountants have increased, but a large majority (41 of 52, or 78.9%) disagree that the benefits of SOX are worth the cost. The greater part of the respondents with an opinion (25 of 43, or 58.1%) state that SOX is not effective in the prevention and detection of fraud in financial statements. And though a strong majority (46 of 52, or 88.5%) agrees that SOX should be modified, 38 of 52 (or 73.1%) disagree that it should be eliminated entirely, while the other 13 (or 25%) do believe that SOX should be completely discarded. These responses appear to support the null hypothesis. However, they do infer that the alternative hypothesis, that SOX is effective in the prevention and detection of fraud in financial statements, is possible if the proper revisions to SOX are instituted.

In evaluating the survey responses and reading through the comments, some frustration is evident concerning the issues of SOX. Executives feel the aggravation due to the increased time and effort required to comply with SOX, especially Section 404 on internal control. The cost of complying with Section 404 of SOX is also a source of annoyance and consternation for the members of management. One CFO feels that SOX was necessary, but was completed in haste and overextended as to its requirements and regulations. This same CFO also feels that SOX is hindering the competitive edge of U.S. corporations because foreign companies do not have to invest the time, the money, and the other resources necessary in order to comply with SOX. Several of the executives feel that it is the responsibility of management to set the tone and encourage compliance with the rules and regulations instituted to prevent fraud. One went so far as to respond that SOX will not in itself prevent accounting irregularities. One CFO appears very frustrated, and feels that SOX is deterring company creativity and innovation, as well as discouraging the formation of new public companies, especially those of smaller size and revenue.

The dissatisfaction of some of the CPAs originates from their opinion that the AICPA was capable of handling the issues that arose, and that the intervention of Congress was unnecessary. One CPA feels that the top accounting firms had caused the problems, but that the small accounting firms are now required to bear the burden of repairing the damage.

As to whether differences in opinions could be ascertained between executives employed by public as opposed to private companies, little distinction is evident. The responses were very similar for almost all the questions. This seems to indicate that even though SOX was written to address the issues specifically brought by publicly traded companies, both public and private companies are experiencing its effects.

As with the unpaired t test and the chi square test, the selection of subjects for the survey is a threat to internal and external validity. Because the concentration of respondents was CPAs and CFOs or CAOs, differing replies could have been received if alternate groups had been questioned. Also, the assumption has been made that those choosing to respond to the survey, of the several hundred that were distributed, are a representative sample of the population as a whole. And as with the statistical analysis testing, responses may vary as time moves forward to when the regulations and compliances of SOX have been instituted for more than just a few years.

In summary, the survey responses and comments from all respondents demonstrate that some irritation and frustration is exhibited with SOX, the changes it necessitates, and the costs of compliance with the legislation. The majority of survey participants feel that the benefits of SOX are not worth the costs, that SOX is not effective in the prevention and detection of fraud in financial statements, and that changes to the legislation are required if it is to be successful. These reactions would appear to support the null hypothesis, that SOX is not effective in the prevention and detection of fraud in financial statements. However, the responses also indicate that despite its flaws,

SOX has the potential to be useful, provided that appropriate modifications are implemented.

Costs of Compliance with SOX

Many comments have been introduced and references made as to the expenditures required to comply with the SOX regulations. The most costly section of SOX is Section 404, which requires an audit report on the adequacy of the internal controls of a public company. Because of this, George Banks, partner in the Dallas office of national accounting firm Grant Thornton, states that "it is safe to say that the time we spend on auditing public companies has fully doubled" (Deener, 2005, p. 2). As a result of this new requirement for an internal controls audit, "the best estimates for the cost of an internal controls audit is at least $150,000 for the smallest companies. At a large company, the bill might run as much as $10 million" (Deener, 2005, p. 2).

Financial Executives International, an organization of policy-makers with 15,000 members, surveyed 217 public companies with revenues of $5 billion or more, and the response was that "the average cost of complying with the new [Section 404] rules was $4.36 million. Outside auditor fees alone soared 58 percent over initial estimates" (Milbourn, 2005, p. 2). Texas Regional Bancshares claims that "the company's audit fees grew 35% just to get ready to meet the requirements of Section 404" (Krantz, 2005, p. 7). Ramtron International Corporation earned $3.3 million in the first nine months of 2004. Without the costs of SOX compliance, "net income would have been 10 percent more" (Beebe, 2005, p. 1). The situation at First Tennessee Bank in Chattanooga is similar in that "Sarbanes-Oxley cost its parent company about $15 million to put into place" (Pare, 2005, p. 1).

In response to the large costs of SOX compliance, some public companies are going private. The American Education Corporation has estimated that going private will "save the company about $320,000" (Mecoy, 2005, p. 1) in SOX compliance costs. Pioneer Oil and Gas is planning a reverse stock split in order to reduce shareholders for the purpose of deregistering with the SEC. The company estimates that "the annual compliance costs will increase for Pioneer Oil and Gas by at least $250,000 annually. This is more than the Company's historical average yearly profits over the last eight years" (PR Newswire Association LLC, 2005/2, p. 1). Lincoln Logs Limited has decided to become less public in response to the additional accounting services required by SOX, which cost over $200,000 in 2004 (Higgins, 2005). Canterbury Consulting Group, Incorporated plans to file a Certification and Notice of Termination with the SEC, resulting in the company being delisted from the Over the Counter Bulletin Board. The company cites "increasing financial disclosure and corporate governance costs in light of the regulatory environment following the Sarbanes-Oxley Act of 2002" (Business Wire, 2005/2, p. 1). The company has estimated the costs at over $200,000 per year "to remain a registered public company, from which we derive very little benefit at a time in our history in which we are trying to return to profitability" (Business Wire, 2005/2, p. 1).

These are just a few of the companies that have voiced their difficulties with the costs required to comply with Section 404 of SOX. But it is a representative sample of the dollar amounts involved as well as the sources of the costs, and the solutions of some of the public companies that must abide by the SOX requirements.

Costs of Financial Statement Restatements

Another set of costs associated with this study relate to the financial statement restatements. This is especially significant as restatements due to faulty earnings recognition reached a high in 2005, more than 50 percent higher than the number reached in 2004 (International Herald Tribune, 2006). Besides the man hours required to recalculate and reformulate the financial statements as necessitated by the discovery of accounting errors requiring correction or adjustment, other tangible and intangible costs exist.

Subsequent to the restatement, the market price of the stock of a company generally decreases. In a study conducted by Mason (2005), it was discovered that "firms with the worst earnings quality (measured as the magnitude of accruals) prior to restatement…experience more negative stock returns after the restatement" (p. 2). Hribar and Jenkins (2003) also found that "on average, accounting restatements lead to both decreases in expected future earnings and increases to the firm's cost of equity capital" (p.1). In addition, Salavei and Moore (2004) examined different motivations behind restatements, and realized that "mismanagement has a negative effect on the market response to restatements for all reasons" (p.1).

These negative market effects were strongly evidenced following the 2001 financial statement restatement of Enron, in which the "impact of this restatement was enormous as Enron's stock dropped 91%" (Lerach, 2004, p. 1). WorldCom experienced a similar fate in response to its 2001 restatement when its stock prices fell "more than 98 percent from their all time high" (Ulick, 2002, p. 2). However, in contrast to these two companies and the general findings, Freddie Mac announced pursuant to the financial statement restatement that the agency published in 2003 that "the restatement did not affect the fundamental strength of Freddie Mac's balance sheet" (Freddie Mac, 2003, p. 2).

Another aspect of the costs incurred when stock decreases is the effect on investors as well as companies. The Government Accounting Office (GAO) reported that "financial statements…not only shake investor confidence but also cost investors billions of dollars in stock value as companies' market prices plummet after the restatements" (Baue, 2002, p. 1). Sarbanes agreed, stating "investors have suffered significant financial harm when the public companies in which they invested misrepresented their financial condition and later restated their financial statements" (Baue, 2002, p. 1).

The costs of financial statement restatements appear for the most part to encompass the tangible cost of declines in stock value, for both companies and investors. The intangible effect of loss of investor confidence also transpires with the occurrence of financial statement restatements, a major concern of Congress and rationale behind the creation of SOX.

Summary of Findings, Analysis, and Evaluation

The statistical analyses indicate that in 61% to 65% of the categories examined, the null hypothesis is supported and SOX is thus not effective in the prevention and detection of fraud in financial statements. And though this is a slim majority, it is still decidedly a majority of cases. The survey suggests that the benefits of SOX are not worth the costs, and it is not effective in the prevention and detection of fraud in financial statements. And though the potential of SOX exists if revisions are implemented, the survey results once again appear to support the null hypothesis.

To expand upon this, the conclusion can be made that SOX should not be eliminated; however, it is also not as effective as it could be. Congress, the AICPA, or the PCAOB does not have to begin anew to create an entirely original piece of legislation or set of regulations, but at the very least modifications should be completed to decrease the costs and limit the time expended by companies in order to comply with SOX. SOX appears to be capable of accomplishing some of the objectives of the legislation, such as further regulating public companies and assisting in the improvement of investor confidence by virtue of these regulations, but falls short of providing effective fraud prevention and detection in financial statements.

In Chapter Five, a summary of this study, the findings, and the resulting conclusions will be presented. Also, the discussion of investor confidence will continue, as will the presentation of further public commentary on SOX, including the aftermath of the legislation. The effectiveness of SOX in the prevention and detection of fraud in financial statements will be visited one last time, and suggestions for further studies will be offered.

CHAPTER FIVE: SUMMARY, CONCLUSIONS, AND RECOMMENDATIONS

The study detailed in the previous four chapters was commenced for the purpose of evaluating the effectiveness of SOX in the prevention and detection of fraud in financial statements. The investigation has undertaken quantitative as well as qualitative analyses, and enough information was gathered and analyzed to form a conclusion.

A brief summary of the information and procedures contained in this study follows. Also included are implications of the results of the study, as well as recommendations for further examination.

General Overview

SOX was signed into law by President Bush in July of 2002. SOX was the response by Congress to the fraudulent accounting scandals that led to the collapse of Enron in 2001 and WorldCom, Adelphia Communications, and Global in early 2002. SOX emphasizes several relevant issues, including the limitation of services offered by independent auditors, responsibilities involved in corporate governance, the adequacy of internal controls, the enhancement of corporate disclosure, personal accountability of management, protection for whistleblowers, and conflicts of interest which have been unduly influencing the opinions of securities analysts.

One of the main objectives in the attempt by SOX to avert the accounting disasters that occurred in 2001 and 2002 is to prevent and detect fraud in financial statements. Other central questions to be addressed by the research involve the determination of whether the costs required to be expended by public companies is worth the benefits provided by SOX, and whether a return in investor confidence is apparent as a result of the regulations of SOX. Also at issue is whether Congress is qualified to have provided a solution to the problems of accounting fraud.

Two statistical analyses, the unpaired t test and the chi square test, were utilized to determine the effectiveness of SOX in the prevention and detection of fraud in financial statements. Published reports became the source of the data for the study, as raw data were not easily accessible. These reports included the reports by the CFTF to President Bush, the enforcement statistics reported on the SEC website, the Reports on Administrative Proceedings established by the SEC, and the reports on financial statement restatements by Huron Corporation. In addition, a survey of eight questions was distributed to various CPAs and corporate executives across the U.S. in order to obtain opinions of those directly involved in the implementation of the directives of SOX.

The findings of the analyses and the survey responses were revealed in Chapter Four. Though the conclusions were not overwhelming, a distinct majority of results indicated that no significant difference exists between pre-SOX and post-SOX statistics, suggesting that SOX is not effective in the prevention and detection of fraud in financial statements. The surveys support the null hypothesis as well by concluding, through a majority of responses, that the benefits of SOX are not worth the costs, and it is not effective in the prevention and detection of fraud in financial statements. However, the survey results also state that SOX should be revised or amended, but not eliminated entirely.

Methodology

A complete description of the methodology utilized in the study is contained in Chapter Three. To briefly summarize, a quantitative methodology was selected to examine the data collected for the purpose of forming a conclusion as to the effectiveness of SOX in the prevention and detection of fraud in financial statements. Statistical instrumentation, specifically the unpaired t test and the chi square test, were selected as the best techniques to perform the assessments of the data.

The correlational design was established to be the most effectual, as the data in the study were to be examined as reported, and not manipulated. The analysis thus developed the relationship between the data and the enactment of SOX, statistically determining if the number of enforcements prior to SOX was greater than, less than, or the same as the number of enforcements subsequent to SOX.

A qualitative methodology was also undertaken by use of the survey. The survey demonstrated a correlational design as well, examining the opinions of SOX in relation to the effectiveness of SOX in the prevention and detection of fraud in financial statements. In addition, the responses addressed the issues of cost versus benefit of SOX, and the necessity of amendment or elimination of SOX. Other elements of both the quantitative and qualitative methodology are the subjects, the instrumentation, and the procedures.

Subjects

For the statistical analysis performed in the study, the subjects were actually data sets. Internet searches were conducted to unearth information concerning SEC actions and proceedings, as well as financial statement problems. As a consequence, the four reports, the CFTF reports, the website enforcement statistics, the Reports on

Administrative Proceedings, and the financial statement restatement reports, were assessed as very relevant to the issue at hand, and thus utilized in the study.

The survey subjects were also selected via the Internet. Various CPAs across the country were targeted from CPA association websites, while the corporate executives were chosen from a corporate information website designed primarily as a marketing tool. The executives represented all sizes of companies, as well as public companies whose securities trade on each of the major exchanges, and private companies. The responses number 52, and represent a decent cross section of all to whom the surveys were distributed.

Instrumentation

After much examination, as detailed in Chapter Three, the unpaired t test was selected as the most effective type of statistical instrumentation to analyze the subject data in order to determine if the pre-SOX values were different from the post-SOX values. The important assumptions and qualifications were fulfilled in order to determine that the unpaired t test would be a sufficient method to employ.

Additional verification of the test results was desired, so another statistical instrument, the chi square test, was selected to analyze the data as well. The chi square test is a non-parametric test, but it is also a test of statistical significance which would be able to determine the difference, if any, between pre-SOX figures and post-SOX figures.

To include the human aspect concerning SOX, an eight-question survey was ascertained to be a valuable instrument capable of qualitatively measuring the effectiveness of SOX. The survey, a copy of which can be found in Appendix H, was distributed to almost 500 CPAs and corporate executives, resulting in 52 responses.

Procedures

The procedures were implemented in Chapter Four. The unpaired t test was run on the two sets of data, the pre-SOX data and the post-SOX data, in each of the 20 categories. The tests were run at least twice to ensure accuracy. The same procedure was performed with the chi square test, but on 18 of the categories, as two of the categories contained zero values, which eliminates calculation by the chi square test. Again the tests were run at least two times to verify the outcomes. The results of both tests were evaluated, as displayed in the tables in Chapter Four, in terms of the significance of the difference between the pre-SOX data and the post-SOX data.

The surveys were emailed via the computer to the CPAs and executives selected. The replies were then separated by type of respondent, and for the executives by type of company, in order to evaluate the feedback.

Results

The results were consequently displayed in Chapter Four. In summary, the unpaired t test indicated that seven of the 20 tests displayed some kind of significant difference between the pre-SOX data and the post-SOX data. However, 65% of the tests run indicate that no significance difference exists between the two sets of numbers. The operation of the chi square test resulted in eight of the 18 tests displaying a significant difference between pre-SOX and post-SOX data, but in one of the eight categories, the mean of the pre-SOX data was actually higher than the mean of the post-SOX data, indicating that SOX was less effective. This category was felt to be in support of the null hypothesis. Accordingly, 61% of the chi square tests run showed no significant difference between the data sets.

The majority of the respondents to the survey agree that SOX has changed the way that accountants perform audits, and the way companies perform accounting tasks. However, 78.9% feel that the benefits of SOX are not worth the costs, and 58.1% of those with an opinion feel that SOX is not effective in the prevention and detection of fraud in financial statements. While 88.5% of the respondents agree that SOX should be amended, 73.1% do not want to entirely eliminate it.

Conclusion

A synopsis of the conclusion would have to begin with a restatement of the null and alternative hypotheses. The null hypothesis affirms that SOX is not effective in the prevention and detection of fraud in financial statements, while the alternative hypothesis states that SOX is effective in the prevention and detection of fraud in financial statements. Any discussion of the conclusion would have to include the selection of the hypothesis that best fits the results of the statistical analyses as well as the survey responses.

Statistical Analysis Conclusion

The majority of the results of both of the statistical analysis tests, the unpaired t test and the chi square test, support the conclusion offered by the null hypothesis. In 61% to 65% of the tests run, the results indicate that no significance difference is evident between pre-SOX data and post-SOX data. This would indicate that SOX has made little or no difference in the prevention and detection of fraud in financial statements.

Peripheral applications of the conclusion would also indicate that because SOX appears to have failed at one of the major objectives of the legislation, it would thus follow that the benefits of SOX are not then worth the costs of implementation. Also it may be inferred that investor confidence would not be fully restored by SOX due to the inability of the legislation in reaching the goal of preventing and detecting fraud. Another allegation may be that Congress has indeed failed in the intention to prevent further accounting scandals.

Survey Conclusion

The responses received through the survey indicate that SOX is not effective in the prevention and detection of fraud in financial statements, and it should be amended but not eliminated entirely. These reactions do appear to support the null hypothesis, as well as suggest that SOX is not as effective as it could be in deterring the occurrence of fraud in financial statements.

The survey results also decided by majority vote that the costs of SOX outweigh the benefits of the legislation. This would furthermore suggest a failure of SOX to be useful overall, thus defeating the other purpose of increasing investor confidence as a result of the limited success of the legislation. Once again the conclusion suggests an unsuccessful attempt by Congress to produce a piece of legislation that was true to the intended objectives.

Theoretical Understanding

The results of the study support the null hypothesis, that SOX is not effective in the prevention and detection of fraud in financial statements. However, because the statistical results display only a slight majority toward this bent, and the survey results demonstrate a desire to amend but not eliminate SOX, the inference can be postulated that SOX may assert some effectiveness, but the legislation is not as effective as is possible.

Congress spent many months and interviewed many witnesses during the process of devising this legislation. However, the study results indicate that SOX is not quite performing as intended, directing the reader to the understanding that financial statement fraud is still occurring, and to the possibility that it cannot ever be legislated or eliminated. Several of the survey respondents as well as other sources previously quoted, such as Dushkin, Ruder, Scherer and Francis, and the Treadway Commission, voiced such a sentiment. As a consequence, investor confidence may again still be in jeopardy. The conclusions cause one to wonder what will work if SOX has, at least in part, failed.

Alternative Explanations of the Findings

Statistical Findings

The statistical data were drawn from two sources. One source was the number of SEC enforcement proceedings occurring over several years, prior to and subsequent to the passage of SOX. However, the SEC was one government agency that experienced the effects of the collapse of Enron, WorldCom, and others, and has thus been subject to some instability since that time. SEC Chairman Harvey Pitt, who took office on August 3, 2001, resigned November 5, 2002 directly as a result of the accounting scandals. William Donaldson, who succeeded Pitt on February 18, 2003, resigned in June, 2005, to be replaced by Christopher Cox, who took office on August 3, 2005. This state of flux, as well as the public pressure caused by the demise of Enron and other companies, may have impeded or at least affected the performance of the SEC enforcement duties subsequent to the passage of SOX.

The other source of data was financial statement restatements. An alternative explanation relating to this source as well as the SEC enforcement proceedings source is that the majority of companies are not involved in reportable fraudulent activities. The COSO report found that "companies committing financial statement fraud were relatively small" (Beasley, Carcello, & Hermanson, 1999). One could possibly conclude that of course no difference in the data would exist because the majority was not committing fraud, either prior to SOX or subsequent to SOX.

Survey Findings

Much of the dissatisfaction over SOX reported by the survey respondents concerned Section 404 of the legislation, which specifies audit procedures required on internal control processes. Complying with the new standards promulgated by SOX has been a costly and time-consuming experience for many of those surveyed as well as those quoted in the Cost section in Chapter Four.

The level of this frustration with Section 404 may have influenced some of the opinions of the survey respondents on other sections of the legislation. Some strong negative feelings were voiced concerning this segment of SOX, leading one respondent to conclude that "this is possibly the biggest and worst modification of securities law since it was enacted" (see Appendix I). Most respondents agree that SOX should be revised, while some even went so far as to agree that it should be completely discarded. The possible implication is that if Section 404 were amended or eliminated, then SOX may indeed be a more effective piece of legislation.

Limitations

The extent of the limitations of any study is very important, and should be addressed during the summation of the study. Therefore, the limitations discussed in Chapter Three should be revisited.

SOX has been in existence for only a little over three years. Evaluating the effectiveness of the legislation may be imperfect due to the minimal amount of data available during the early stages of SOX. As the years go by and SOX is in existence for a longer period of time, the results of future analyses may indicate a different conclusion. Also, the bias of the author of the study as well as the bias of the readers of the resulting dissertation may create different interpretations by each as to the outcomes of the study, and must be kept in mind when examining the conclusions.

Assumptions have been made that the data scrutinized in the study and the statistical methods engaged are the most appropriate in assessing the effectiveness of SOX. Other data and other methods may be more appropriate, and indeed create a different conclusion if employed.

Implications

The most obvious implication of SOX not being effective in the prevention and detection of fraud in financial statements is that fraud is still occurring. Parvaz (2005) agrees, saying "there's a never-ending ticker tape of appalling corporate behavior – companies lying to their employees, stealing from their investors, shortchanging employee pension plans while paying huge salaries to their CEOs, and on and on" (p.1). For instance, in March of 2003, the SEC filed a lawsuit against HealthSouth Corporation, a provider of outpatient surgery, diagnostic imaging, and rehabilitative healthcare services, as well as the CEO and chairman of HealthSouth Corporation, alleging the perpetration of a $1.4 billion accounting fraud (CNN Money, 2003, p.1). Also, in September of 2005, three headlines appeared in just one issue of an ACFE fraud newsletter stating that "two former Westar executives convicted of fraud, Qwest

116

executives lose bid to get lawsuit claims dismissed, skateboard executive pleads guilty to securities fraud" (Fraud Info, 2005, pp. 1-2). The success of SOX appears to definitely be in question.

Another implication that begs to be addressed is the notion that Congress is not equipped to legislate fraud or to regulate the accounting profession. Fox (2005) agrees, claiming that "the belief that legislators, regulators, and judges can somehow put an end to corporate wrongdoing is persistent but mistaken" (p.2). Former SEC commissioner Grundfest is also in agreement, explaining that "it is human nature at some point in commercial dealings to go too far, to try to take advantage" (Fox, p.2). However, Oxley defends government action in this situation because "the accounting industry has been found to be incapable of regulating itself" (Distefano, 2005, p.1).

The restoration of investor confidence is one of the major objectives of SOX. The conclusion of this study would indicate that it has not occurred, which could have a devastating effect on the securities market. However, investors appear nonplussed by internal control weaknesses disclosed under Section 404 of SOX. "56 percent of the companies disclosing material weaknesses in their internal controls saw their stock price increase at the end of the day in which the disclosure occurred" (Business Wire, 2005/1, p.1). Apparently investors are themselves dismissing SOX. "Educated, active investors, particularly institutional investors, clearly understand the relative importance of a minor control issue that a company was urged to disclose by its auditor" (Business Wire, 2005/1, p.2). In opposition, Edward Knight, general counsel of The Nasdaq Stock Market Incorporated argues that "Sarbanes-Oxley is accomplishing its main goal: reassuring jittery investors that the stock market waters are safe again" (Reisinger, 2005,

117

p.16). However, Knight counters this by stating "it's quite possible the institutional forces could have brought a lot of this change [anyway]" (Reisinger, p.17).

The need for revising the legislation itself is another implication that has resulted from this study. HealthSouth Corporation CEO Richard Scrushy, upon being the first CEO indicted for fraud under SOX, claimed that the legislation "was unconstitutional on its face because it was too vague to give adequate notice as to what particular conduct was unlawful and provides no limitation on the discretion of government officials to prevent arbitrary and capricious enforcement" (Richardson, 2005, p.1). Section 404 of SOX has provided much consternation among corporate executives, so much so that "companies say they agree strong internal controls are necessary, but Section 404 is overkill and they want it amended" (Ambrose, 2005, p.2). In addition, 46 of the 52 survey respondents strongly agree or agree that SOX should be amended. It appears that some sort of revision is in order.

As discussed in Chapter Four, several public companies are or have considered going private, which alters the control, capitalization, and ownership of the company, or going dark, which involves deregistering with the SEC (Norman, 2005). Thousands of public companies succeed in the U.S., but in 2003 alone, 79 went private and 127 went dark (Norman). According to attorney Thomas Magill, "hundreds more could soon follow" (Norman, p.1). The foremost reason given for the majority of the companies, especially the small, public corporations, that have made these changes since 2002 is to eliminate the exorbitant costs of complying with SOX (Paul, 2005). The implication to be made in this situation is the possibility that many, many more public companies will go private or go dark, causing serious problems for the securities market and the U.S. economy.

However, delisting with the stock exchanges may not save companies from the costs and rigors of complying with SOX. New York and California are "considering legislation to extend the requirements of Sarbanes-Oxley, or SOX, to private companies and nonprofits" (Balousek, 2005, p.1). To that end, California has already passed Senate Bill 1262, titled the Nonprofit Integrity Act, which went into effect on January 1, 2005 and addresses such issues as public disclosures of the financial statements, formation of an audit committee within the board of directors, and requirements for contracts with fundraisers. On the other hand, "some companies are complying because their big-company clients are asking them to" (Walker, 2005, p.2). Fitch Ratings Agency, known since 1913 as a premier financial statistics company, believes that "voluntary adoption of Sarbanes-Oxley provisions will strengthen governance through increased accountability that can lend significant credibility to a hospital or health care system's financial reporting" (Business Wire, 2005/3, p.1). These sentiments, along with the agreement of the majority of the survey respondents that SOX should not be eliminated entirely, form the implication that SOX does have some merit not only concerning public companies, but for private and nonprofit companies as well.

Corporate transparency of financial statements and improved corporate governance reflect another implication issue addressed by the study. SOX was enacted as a direct result of the lack of transparency in the financial transactions embraced by Enron, which caused the collapse of the company and the financial demise of many of the investors of the company. Thus the intent of SOX is to provide for more corporate transparency and better investor protection. Tapscott and Ticoll (2003) uphold the importance of transparency, stating that "transparency and corporate values enhance market value" (p. xiv). However, they also conclude that "the Sarbanes-Oxley Act of 2002, prompted by the Enron meltdown, is a step in the right direction, but it falls short in the critical reforms necessary for accountability" (p. 247). Former SEC chief accountant Lynn Turner, when questioned concerning the status of corporate governance in the post-Enron years, replied that "we certainly have seen some improvements in governance, but we've also seen some areas of no improvement, and some areas where things have gone backwards" (International Herald Tribune, 2006, p.1). Again the concern is expressed that SOX is not as effective as it should be in order to accomplish the goals established for the legislation.

Alternatively, other people believe that SOX is doing well. Former SEC chairman Donaldson (2005) asserts that "the Act has effected dramatic change across corporate America and beyond, and is helping to reestablish investor confidence in the integrity of corporate disclosures and financial reporting" (p.1). Alan Greenspan, Chairman of the Board of Governors of the Federal Reserve System, is also in agreement, stating that "I am surprised that the Sarbanes-Oxley Act, so rapidly developed and enacted, has functioned as well as it has" (Walters, 2005, p.2). Oxley himself has responded to critics, saying "the system really does work," basing his remarks on the recoveries that have occurred in the stock market in recent years (Distefano, 2005, p.1).

In addition, the influences of the regulations of SOX are reaching overseas to Europe. The European Union and the European Small Business Association are encouraging the revision of audit rules for public companies. The draft of the new

European Parliament and Council Directive seeks to "clarify the duties and ethics of statutory auditors and audit firms" (Europe Information Service, 2005, p.1). The provisions of the directive have been compared to sections of SOX, indicating that some of the policies of SOX have been found to have merit within the European community.

The implications of the study are varied, and are mixed as to their support of SOX. These assorted viewpoints sustain the conclusion drawn in the study, that SOX does have some value concerning transparency, investor confidence, and company perceptions. However, the legislation is still not as effective as it could be concerning fraud prevention and detection, and the cost efficiency of SOX is seriously lacking in comparison to the benefits that are provided to complying companies.

Recommendations for Further Research

The most obvious recommendation for further research is to re-evaluate the effectiveness of SOX in the prevention and detection of fraud in financial statements after it has been in existence for more than just over three years. The study should be recreated once the legislation has been continuously mandating corporate compliance for five years or even ten years. The use of different statistical information and/or alternate instrumentation for the analysis in this subsequent investigation could also be selected. The results may change dramatically, or may remain the same.

Another possibility for further study would be a focus on Section 404 of SOX. A comprehensive analysis of costs versus benefits regarding Section 404 would be valuable for the creators of SOX to determine if this segment of the legislation should itself be amended or eliminated entirely.

For that matter, a cost versus benefits examination of the entire SOX legislation would be advisable as well. This could assist lawmakers in deciding whether or not it would be advantageous to repeal SOX in total, even though the majority of those responding to the survey in this study were not in favor of such a drastic measure.

Other issues to be investigated include the capability of the accounting profession to legislate and regulate itself, as well as the advantage provided foreign companies that are not required to abide by the regulations of SOX. Another subject of great interest is the number of public companies that have delisted with the SEC due to the rigors of SOX conformity, and the extent to which this number is increasing or declining. Extension of the Coates study concerning the impact of SOX on the corporate ethical climate as well as extension of the Zhang study of the economic consequences of SOX, both discussed in Chapter Two, could be done to encompass more than the one to three post-SOX years influencing these two evaluations. A more thorough study could also be completed concerning the effects of a more ethical corporate climate and greater corporate financial transparency on the instances of fraud in financial statements.

Summary

SOX has been called the most important piece of financial legislation to be presented to public companies since the SEC Act of 1934 (Pellet, 2003). A crucial requirement then exists to examine the legislation to verify whether or not the stated objectives are being accomplished.

This study has striven to make this very determination concerning one major objective, which is the effectiveness of SOX in the prevention and detection of fraud in financial statements. Through the statistical analyses and survey responses presented in this examination, the determination has been made that though SOX may have some redeemable qualities and possess the potential for success concerning its major objectives, SOX is not effective in the prevention and detection of fraud in financial statements.

References

Albrecht, W. S. (2003). *Recent developments in accounting education.* Retrieved March

25, 2004, from

http://www.nasba.org/NASBAfiles.nsf/Lookup/Albrecht/$file/Albrecht.pdf

Ambrose, E. (2005, January 30). The Baltimore Sun Eileen Ambrose column. *The*

Baltimore Sun. Retrieved February 2, 2005 from

http://www.highbeam.com/library/doc3.asp?DOCID=1G1:127951259&num=1&c

trlInfo=Round17%3AProd%3ASR%3AResult&ao=&FreePremium=BOTH

American Institute of Certified Public Accountants (AICPA). (1977, June). *The*

commission on auditors' responsibilities: Report, conclusions, and

recommendations. Retrieved September 26, 2004, from

http://www.biz.colostate.edu/qfr/references/CommissiononAuditorsResponsibility

.pdf

American Institute of Certified Public Accountants (AICPA). (1995, November). *AICPA*

mission statement. Retrieved January 25, 2005, from

http://www.aicpa.org/about/mission.htm

American Institute of Certified Public Accountants (AICPA). (2004). *The CPA and fraud*

detection. Retrieved April 7, 2004, from http://finance.pro2net.com/x12816.xml

Aurora Public Schools. (2004). *Glossary.* Retrieved January 26, 2005, from

http://www.aps.k12.co.us/district-into/finances/budget/Glossary/glossary.htm

Bachman, J. (2004). Business watercooler stories. *AP Online.* Retrieved February 13,

2004 from http://www.highbeam.com/library/doc3.asp?DOCID=1P1:91021846

Balhoff, W. E. (2002, March 14). *Prepared statement of Mr. William E. Balhoff, CPA,*
CFE, chairman, Executive Committee AICPA Public Company Practice Section,
senior audit director, Postlethwaite & Netterville, A.P.A.C. Retrieved August 14,
2002, from http://banking.senate.gov/02_03hrg/031402/balhoff.htm

Ballweiser, W. (2002). *Accounting and auditing: Interaction in the regulation and*
research domains. Retrieved March 25, 2004, from http://www.rwp.bwl.uni-
muenchen.de/download/Kopenhagen02.pdf

Balousek, M. (2005, May 1). Private companies, nonprofits can't ignore SOX: Federal
law mandates document retention, other internal controls. *Wisconsin State*
Journal. Retrieved May 3, 2005 from
http://www.highbeam.com/library/doc3.asp?ctrlInfo=Round91%3AProd%3ADO
C%3APring&DOCID=1G1:132060438&print=yes

Baue, W. (2002, November 6). *GAO report says financial restatements cost investors*
billions. Retrieved August 26, 2005, from
http://www.socialfunds.com/news/article.cgi/960.html

Beasley, M.S., Carcello, J.V., & Hermanson, D.R. (1999, May). COSO's new fraud
study: what it mans for CPAs. *Journal of Accountancy, 187*, 12. Retrieved
September 17, 2005, from http://www.rowan.edu/business/faculty/byrd/Fraud.htm

Beebe, P. (2005, February 16). Association complains of new financial reporting
regulation. *The Gazette.* Retrieved February 18, 2005, from
http://www.highbeam.com/library/doc3.asp?DOCID=1G1:128751265&num=1&c
trlInfo=Round16%3AProd%3ASR%sAResult&ao=&FreePremium=BOTH

Beresford, D. R. (2002, February 26). *Prepared statement of Mr. Dennis R. Beresford, chairman, Financial Accounting Standards Board, 1987-1997*. Retrieved August 14, 2004, from http://banking.senate.gov/02_02hrg/022602/beresfrd.htm

Berlau, J. (2004, February 2). *Sarbanes-Oxley is business disaster: Passage of the Sarbanes-Oxley Corporate Reform Act was supposed to stop corporate abuses, but instead it has strangled small business and slowed job growth*. Retrieved June 20, 2004, from http://articles.findarticles.com/p/articles/mi_m1571/is_2004_Feb_2/ai_112723160/print

Berman, N., DeValerio, G., Pease, P. A., Tabacco Jr., J. J., Burt III, C. O., & Pucillo, M. J. (2003). *Corporate execs mixed on Sarbanes-Oxley impact*. Retrieved April 7, 2004, from http://www.bermanesq.com/News/NewsItemxasp?titleid=126

Biggs, J. H. (2002, February 27). *Prepared statement of Mr. John H. Biggs, chairman, president and CEO, Teachers' Insurance and Annuity Association-College Retirement Equities Fund (TIAA-CREF)*. Retrieved August 14, 2004, from http://banking.senate.gov/02_02hrg/022702/biggs.htm

Blue Ribbon Committee. (1999). *Report and recommendations of the Blue Ribbon Committee on improving the effectiveness of corporate audit committees*. Retrieved August 29, 2004, from http://www.nyse.com/pdfs/blueribb.pdf

Bowman, T. A. (2002, March 20). *Prepared statement of Mr. Thomas A. Bowman, president and CEO, Association for Investment Management and Research*. Retrieved August 14, 2002, from http://banking.senate.gov/02_03hrg/032002/bowman.htm

126

Bowsher, C. A. (2002, March 19). *Prepared statement of Mr. Charles A. Bowsher, chairman, Public Oversight Board, Former Comptroller General of the United States*. Retrieved August 14, 2004, from http://banking.senate.gov/02_03hrg/031902/bowsher.htm

Brand, M. (2004, January 13). *Analysis: Number of companies making revision to their bottom lines rises to new record*. Retrieved January 16, 2004, from http://ask.elibrary.com/getdoc.asp?c=2&oid=12481579&query=SARBANES-OXLEY+ACT+OF=2002&querydocid=1P1:893653

Breeden, R. C. (2002, February 12). *Prepared statement of the Honorable Richard C. Breeden, chairman, Securities and Exchange Commission, 1989-93*. Retrieved August 14, 2004, from http://banking.senate.gov/02_02hrg/021202/breeden.htm

Bush, G. W. (2002/1, January 29). *President delivers state of the Union address*. Retrieved October 3, 2004, from http://www.whitehouse.gov/news/releases/2002/01/20020129-11.html

Bush, G. W. (2002/2, July 30). *Statement by the President*. Retrieved October 3, 2004, from http://www.whitehouse.gov/news/releases/2002/07/20020730-10.html

Business Editors. (2004, February 10). *The world's largest anti-fraud association says: Most companies get an "F" in fraud prevention; ACFE one-day course offered in Long Beach*. Retrieved June 20, 2004, from http://articles.findarticles.com/p/articles/mi_m)EIN/is_2004_Feb_10/ai_11311029 8/print

Business Wire. (2005/1, March 8). *Compliance week analyzes stock market's reaction to internal control weakness, deficiency disclosures.* Retrieved March 9, 2005 from http://www.highbeam.com/library/doc3.asp?ctrlInfo=Round9j%3AProd%3ADOC53APrint&DOCID=1G1:129898071&print=yes

Business Wire. (2005/2, May 26). *Canterbury plans to deregister its common stock and delist from the OTC Bulletin Board.* Retrieved June 2, 2005, from http://www.highbeam.com/library/docfree.asp?DOCID=1G1:132780412&num=1&ctrlInfo=Round16%3AProd%3ASR%sAResult&ao=&FreePremium=BOTH

Business Wire. (2005/3, August 9). *Fitch: Sarbanes-Oxley and not-for-profit hospitals.* Retrieved August 10, 2005 from http://www.highbeam.com/library/docfree.asp?DOCID=1G1:134966588&ctrlInfo=Round15%AProd%3ADOC%3AResult&ao=&FreePremium=BOTH

Caplan, M. H. (2004, July 22). *Sarbanes-Oxley: Two years of market and investor recovery.* Retrieved August 14, 2004, from http://financialservices.house.gov/media/pdf/072204mc.pdf

CFO, Magazine for Senior Financial Executives. (2003, May). *"You are the guardians" - as chairman of the Securities and Exchange Commission from 1993 to 2001, Arthur Levitt warned that inadequate disclosure and the conflicts of interest entangling corporate America with its auditors and analysis could ultimately damage confidence in the capital markets.* Retrieved June 20, 2004, from http://articles.findarticles.com/p/articles/mi_m3870/is_6_19/ai_101531493/print

Clayton, R. D., & Mackintosh, T. (2002). *Corporate governance: Avoiding criminal liability under Sarbanes-Oxley*. Retrieved April 7, 2004, from http://library.lp.findlaw.com/articles.file/00318/008546/title/Subject/topic/Corporations%20%20Enterprise%20Law_Director%20%20Officer%20Liability/filename/corporationsenterpriselaw_1_114

CNN Money. (2003, March 19). *HealthSouth cited for $1.4B fraud*. Retrieved September 17, 2005 from http://cnnmoney.cnn.com/2003/03/19/news/companies/healthsouth/

Coates, B. E. (2003). *Rogue corporations, corporate rogues & ethics compliance: The Sarbanes-Oxley Act, 2002*. Retrieved October 3, 2004, from http://www.pamij.com/8-3/pam8-3-6-coates.pdf

Committee of Sponsoring Organizations of the Treadway Commission. (1999, March). *Fraudulent financial reporting: 1987-1997: An analysis of U.S. public companies*. Retrieved September 27, 2004, from http://www.coso.org/publications/FFR_1987_1997.pdf

Connor-Linton, J. (2003, March 22). *Chi square tutorial*. Retrieved June 8, 2005 from http://www.georgetown.edu/faculty/ballc/webtools/web_chi_tut.html.

Copeland, J. E. (2002, March 14). *Prepared statement of Mr. James E. Copeland, CPA, chief executive officer, Deloitte & Touche*. Retrieved August 14, 2004, from http://banking.senate.gov/02_03hrg/031402/copeland.htm

Corporate Fraud Task Force (CFTF). (2003). *First year report to the President*. Retrieved October 13, 2004, from http://www.usdoj.gov/dag/cftf/first_year_report.pdf

129

Coustan, H. (2004, February). *Sarbanes-Oxley: What it means to the marketplace; from support to apprehension, accounting professionals express their thoughts.* Retrieved June 20, 2004, from http://articles.findarticles.com/p/articles/mi_m6280/is_2_197/ai_113304248/print

Dauberman, M. (2004, June 18). *The audit process: A risk-based approach with an emphasis on fraud.* Paper presented at the meeting of the Consideration of Fraud. Woodland Hills, CA.

Davia, H. R. (2000). *Fraud 101: Techniques and strategies for detection.* New York: John Wiley and Sons, Inc.

Davia, H. R., Coggins, P. C., Wideman, J. C., & Kastantin, J. T. (2000). *Accountant's guide to fraud detection and control* (2nd ed.). New York: John Wiley and Sons, Inc.

Deener, W. (2005, April 25). Firms struggle to meet act's requirement. *The Dallas Morning News.* Retrieved April 26, 2005, from http://www.highbeam.com/library/doc3.asp?ctrlInfo=Round91%3AProd%3ADOC%3APrint &DOCID=1G!:131860927&print=yes

Delaney, P. R., Epstein, B. J., Nach, R., & Budak, S. W. (2003). *Wiley GAAP 2004: Interpretation and application of generally accepted accounting principles.* New York: John Wiley & Sons, Inc.

Del Raso, J. V. (2004, July 22). *Statement of Joseph V. Del Raso, Esq., partner, Pepper Hamilton LLP, to the House Financial Services Committee on "Sarbanes-Oxley: Two Years of Market and Investor Recovery".* Retrieved August 14, 2004, from http://financialservices.house.gov/media/pdf/072204jd.pdf

Deputy Attorney General. (2002). *Executive Order 13271 of July 9, 2002*. Retrieved

    January 25, 2005, from http://www.usdoj.gov/dag/cftf/execorder.htm

Dictionary.com. (2000). *Dictionary*. Retrieved April 18, 2004, from

    http://dictionary.reference.com/search?q=limitations

Distefano, J.N. (2005, April 27). Reforms successful, Oxley says. *The Philadelphia*

    Inquirer. Retrieved April 28, 2005 from

    http://www.highbeam.com/library/doc3.asp?ctrlInfo=Round91%3AProd%3ADO

    C%3APrint&DOCID=1G1:131922210&print=yes

Donaldson, W.H. (2005, April 21). *Impact of Sarbanes-Oxley Act: William H.*

    Donaldson: *Congressional Testimony*. Retrieved April 25, 2005 from

    http://www.highbeam.com/library/doc3.asp?ctrlInfo=Round91%3AProd%3ADO

    C%3Aprint&DOCID=1P1:107782505&print=yes

Dushkin Online. (2000). *Accountancy: Fraud and financial statements*. Retrieved May

    25, 2004, from http://www.dushkin.com/text-data/weekly/cm12-25-00.mhtml

Europe Information Service (2005). *Company law: European Parliament due to approve*

    audit directive overhaul. Retrieved September 30, 2005 from

    http://www.highbeam.com/library/doc3.asp?DOCID=1G1:136740071&alert_topi

    c=SARBANES-OXLEY+ACT+OF+2002

Financial Accounting Standards Board (FASB). (2004). *The mission of the Financial*

    Accounting Standards Board. Retrieved January 26, 2005, from

    http://www.fasb.org/facts/facts_about_fasb.pdf

FindLaw. (1999). *Legal Dictionary*. Retrieved January 26, 2005, from

    http://dictionary.lp.findlaw.com/scripts/results.pl?co=dictionary.lp.findlaw.com&t

    opic=6e/6ebc1118feb1b4f89a7955c178bdd5af

Fox, J. (2005, June 27). Calling off the dogs: An era of corporate-crime fighting is

    ending. What's to keep fraudsters from striking again? Fear, and a stock market

    stuck in neutral. *Fortune*. Retrieved June 28, 2005 from

    http://www.highbeam.com/library/doc3asp?DOCID=1G1:133228969&num=2&c

    trlInfo=Round17%3AProd%3ASR%3AResult%ao=&FreePremium=BOTH

Fraud Info. (2005, September 15). *Fraud News Flash*. Retrieved September 17, 2005

    from http://d04.webmail.aol.com/display-message.aspx

Freddie Mac. (2003, November 21). *Freddie Mac announces restatement results*.

    Retrieved August 26, 2005, from

    http://www.freddiemac.com/news/archives/investors/2003/restatement_112103.ht

    ml

Friedman, J. (2002). *The emerging company and the SEC: The significance of the

    Sarbanes-Oxley Act*. Retrieved April 17, 2004, from

    http://www.businessforum.com/SEC01.html

Frieswick, K. (2003, July). *How audits must change: auditors face more pressure to find

    fraud*. Retrieved June 20, 2004, from

    http://articles.findarticles.com/p/articles/mi_m3870/is_9_19/ai_105460795/print

Hahn. (2003). *Paired t-test*. Retrieved April 6, 2005, from

    http://www.ams.sunysb.edu/~hahn/course/minitab/pairedt-test/pairedt.html

Harrington, C. (2003, August). *The new accounting environment: Companies face a paradigm shift in how they conduct business.* Retrieved June 20, 2004, from http://articles.findarticles.com/p/articles/mi_m6280/is_2_196/ai_106390476/print

Herdman, R. K. (2001, December 12). *Testimony concerning recent events relating to Enron Corporation.* Retrieved September 26, 2003, from http://www.sec.gov/news/testimony/121201tsrkh.htm

Higgins, D. (2005, April 4). Honesty costs money. *Times Union.* Retrieved April 6, 2005, from http://www.highbeam.com/library/doc3.asp?ctrlInfo=Round9k%3AProd%3ADOC%3APrint&DOCID=1G1:131145704&print=yes

Hills, R. M. (2002, February 12). *Prepared statement of the Honorable Roderick M. Hills, chairman, Securities and Exchange Commission, 1975-77.* Retrieved August 14, 2004, from http://banking.senate.gov/02_02hrg/021202/hills.htm

Hills, R. M. (2004, July 22). *Statement of the Honorable Roderick M. Hills before the Committee on Financial Services, United States House of Representatives.* Retrieved August 14, 2004, from http://financialservices.house.gov/media/pdf/072204rh.pdf

Hoover's Inc. (2005). *Huron Consulting Group Inc.* Retrieved June, 10, 2005 from http://www.hovers.com/free/co/factsheet.xhtml?&ID=132773&abforward=true

House Financial Services Committee. (2001, December 12). *Joint hearing: The Enron collapse: Impact on investors and financial markets.* Retrieved August 14, 2004, from http://commdocs.house.gov/committees/bank/hba76958.000/hba76958_0.htm

House Financial Services Committee. (2002/1, February 4). *The Enron collapse:*

    Implications to investors and the capital markets. Retrieved August 14, 2004,

    from

    http://commdocs.house.gov/committees/bank/hba77683.000/hba77683_0.htm

House Financial Services Committee. (2002/2, March 13). *H.R. 3763-the Corporate and*

    Auditing Accountability, Responsibility and Transparency Act of 2002. Retrieved

    August 14, 2004, from

    http://commdocs.house.gov/committees/bank/hba78501.000/hab78501_0.htm

House Financial Services Committee. (2002/3, March 20). *H.R. 3763, the Corporate and*

    Auditing Accountability, Responsibility, and Transparency Act of 2002. Retrieved

    August 14, 2004, from

    http://commdocs.house.gov/committees/bank/hba78501.000/hba78501_1.HTM

House Financial Services Committee. (2002/4, April 9). *H.R. 3763, the Corporate and*

    Auditing Accountability, Responsibility and Transparency Act of 2002. Retrieved

    August 14, 2004, from

    http://commdocs.house.gov/committees/bank/hba78501.000/hba78501_2.HTM

House of Representatives. (2002/1, July 11). *Corporate accountability.* Retrieved August

    8, 2004, from http://thomas.loc.gov/cgi-bin/query/C?r107:./temp/~r107DV8edb

House of Representatives. (2002/2, July 25). *Conference report on H.R. 3763, Sarbanes-*

    Oxley Act of 2002. Retrieved August 8, 2004, from http://thomas.loc.gov/cgi-

    bin/C?r107:./temp/~r10704CmMd

Hribar, P., & Jenkins, N. T. (2003, August). *The effect of accounting restatements on earnings revisions and the estimated cost of capital*. Retrieved August 26, 2005, from

http://www.anderson.ucla.edu:8888/acad_unit/accounting/hribar_jenkinssept10.pdf#search='cost%20restatements'

Huron Consulting Group. (2004, February). *2003 annual review of financial reporting matters*. Retrieved February 3, 2005, from

http://www.iasplus.com/resource/huron2003.pdf

Huron Consulting Group. (2005, March 25). *2004 annual review of financial reporting matters: Final report*. Retrieved August 23, 2005, from

http://www.huronconsultinggroup.com/uploadedFiles/Huron_2004_Review%20of%20Financial%20Reporting%20Matters.pdf

International Accounting Standards Board (IASB). (2005). *About us: Mission statement*. Retrieved January 25, 2005, from http://www.iasb.org/about/index.asp

International Herald Tribune. (2006, January 5). *Going backwards after Enron: Lessons from debacle lost*. Retrieved January 7, 2006 from

http://www.highbeam.com/library/doc3.asp?DOCID=1P1:116995277&alert_topic=SARBANES-OXLEY+ACT+OF+2002

Jones, P. (2004). *Single-case statistical analysis: Statistical tools*. Retrieved April 18, 2005, from http://www.unlv.edu/faculty/pjones/singlecase/scsatool.htm

Kam, B. (2002). *Responses on t-test*. Retrieved April 6, 2005, from

http://isb.ri.ccf.org/biomch-l/archives/biomch-l-1999-02/00085.html

Kaplan, A. (1998). *The conduct of inquiry: Methodology for behavioral science.* New
Brunswick: Transaction Publishers.

Keller, S. (2002). *The Sarbanes-Oxley Act of 2002.* Retrieved April 17, 2004, from
http://www.palmerdodge.com/dspSingleArticle.cfm?articleid=466

Kirtley, O. F. (2002, March 14). *Prepared statement of Ms. Olivia F. Kirtley, CPA,
former chair, Board of Directors AICPA (1998-99), retired vice president and
CFO, Vermont American Company.* Retrieved August 14, 2004, from
http://banking.senate.gov/02_03hrg/031402/kirtley.htm

Kisamore, J. (2003). *Two sample t-test assumptions.* Retrieved February 16, 2005, from
http://faculty-staff.ou.edu/K/Jennifer.Kisamore-1/teaching/ttestutor/tsld040.htm

Krantz, M. (2005, March 24). *More finance chiefs are dropping out: Long hours,
burdensome rules fuel high turnover.* Retrieved March 25, 2005, from
http://www.highbeam.com/library/doc3.asp?ctrlInfo=Round9j%3AProd%3ADO
C%3APrint&DOCID=1P1:106727984&print=yes

Kurlantzick, J. (2003, October). *Liar liar: In the race to make money, some American
businesses have been lying their pants off-but is success at any cost really worth
the price?* Retrieved June 20, 2004, from
http://articles.findarticles.com/p/articles/mi_m0DTI/is_10_31/ai_109403729/print

Kwechansky, A. (2003). *Dirty deeds.* Retrieved March 25, 2004, from
http://alextalksbusiness.com/page3.html

Langevoort, D.C. (2002, April 9). *Testimony of Professor Donal C. Langevoort,*
Georgetown University Law Center, before the Committee on Financial Services,
United States House of Representatives, 107th Congress. Retrieved August 14,
2004, from http://financialservices.house.gov/media/pdf/040902dl.pdf

'Lectric Law Library. (2004/1, March). *Fraud, to defraud.* Retrieved January 26, 2005,
from http://www.lectlaw.com/def/f0179.htm

'Lectric Law Library. (2004/2, March). *Initial public offering.* Retrieved January 26,
2005, from http://www.lectlaw.com/def/i045.htm

Legal Definitions. (2004). *Fraud.* Retrieved January 25, 2005, from http://www.legal-
definitions.com/fraud.htm

Lerach, W. S. (2004). *The Enron lawsuit.* Retrieved August 26, 2005, from
http://www.enronfraud.com/

Levitt, A., Jr. (2002, February 12). *Prepared statement of the Honorable Arthur Levitt,*
Jr., chairman, Securities and Exchange Commission, 1993-2000. Retrieved
August 14, 2004, from http://banking.senate.gov/02_02hrg/021202/levitt.htm

Lindberg, D. L., & Beck, F. D. (2004, November 4). *Before and after Enron: CPAs'*
views on auditor independence. Retrieved January 28, 2005, from
http://www.nysscpa.org/cpajournal/2004/1104/essentials/p36.htm

Litan, R. E. (2002, March 14). *Prepared statement of Mr. Robert E. Litan, director,*
Economic Studies Program, The Brookings Institution, Bear, Stearns & Co., Inc.
Retrieved August 14, 2004, from
http://banking.senate.gov/02_03hrg/031402/litan.htm

Mason, R. (2005, April). *Short sellers can see through "creative" (aggressive)*

    accounting practices. Retrieved August 26, 2005, from

    http://www.cos.smu.edu/article/research/research.do/130

McCall, H.C. (2002, March 20). *New York State Comptroller H. Carl McCall Testimony*

    before the Committee on Financial Services, U.S. House of Representatives.

    Retrieved August 14, 2004, from

    http://financialservices.house.gov/media/pdf/032002cm.pdf

McMillan, J. H., & Schumacher, S. (2001). *Research in education: A conceptual*

    introduction (5th ed.). New York: Addison Wesley Longman, Inc..

Mecoy, D. (2005, June 22). Oklahoma City-based education software company seeks

    private status. *The Daily Oklahoman*. Retrieved June 24, 2005, from

    http://www.highbeam.com/library/doc3.asp?DOCID=1G1:133502338&num=1&c

    trlInfo=Round16%3Aprod%sASR%3Aresult&ao=&FreePremium=BOTH

Milbourn, M. A. (2005, April 10). New rules heaping work on companies. *The Orange*

    County Register. Retrieved April 12, 2005, from

    http://www.highbeam.com/library/doc3.asp?ctrlInfo=Round9k%3AProd%3ADO

    C%3APrint&DOCID=1G1:131303234&print=yes

Miller, G. G. (2004/1, September 21). *Letter to Ms. Debbie Yabrof*. Washington, DC.

Miller, R. (2004/2, February 8). The Dallas Morning News Robert Miller column. *The*

    Dallas Morning News. Retrieved February 12, 2004, from

    http://www.highbeam.com/library/doc3asp?DOCID=1G1:113039566

Millstein, I. M. (2002, February 27). *Prepared statement of Mr. Ira M. Millstein, senior partner, Weil, Gotshal and Manges*. Retrieved August 14, 2004, from http://banking.senate.gov/02_02hrg/022702.htm

Mulford, C. W., & Comiskey, E. E. (2002). *The financial numbers game: Detecting creative accounting practices.* New York: John Wiley and Sons, Inc.

National Commission on Fraudulent Financial Reporting. (1987, October). *Report of the National Commission on Fraudulent Financial Reporting.* Retrieved August 5, 2004, from http://www.coso.org/NCFFR.pdf

Nationmaster. (2005). *Encyclopedia: Worldcom.* Retrieved January 30, 2005, from http://www.nationmaster.com/encyclopedia/Worldcom

Needles, Jr., B. E., Anderson, H. R., & Caldwell, J. C. (1981). *Prinicples of accounting* (5th ed.). Boston: Houghton Mifflin Company.

Norman, J. (2005, April 10). Companies 'go dark' to cut compliance costs. *The Orange County Register.* Retrieved April 12, 2005, from http://www.highbeam.com.library.doc3.asp?ctrlInfo=Round9k%3AProd%3ADOC%3APrint&DOCID=1G1:131305801&print=yes

Oklahoma State University. (2004). *Bias in research.* Retrieved April 17, 2004, from http://soil5813.okstate.edu/Bias_in_research2004.htm

O'Malley, S. (2002, March 6). *Prepared statement of Mr. Shaun O'Malley, chair of the 2000 Public Oversight Board Panel on Audit Effectiveness (O'Malley Commission) and former chair, Price Waterhouse LLP.* Retrieved August 14, 2004, from http://banking.senate.gov/02_03hrg/030602/omalley.htm

One Hundred Seventh Congress of the United States of America. (2002, July 23). *To protect investors by improving the accuracy and reliability of corporate disclosures made pursuant to the securities laws, and for other purposes.* Retrieved January 27, 2004, from

http://news.findlaw.com/hdocs/docs/gwbush/sarbanesoxley072302.pdf

Osenberg. (2003). *Statistics guide.* Retrieved April 18, 2005, from

http://www.zoo.ufl.edu/courses/pcb4044/2003Spring/stats.pdf

O'Sullivan, K. (2004, November). *Do as I do.* Retrieved January 27, 2005, from

http://www.cfo.com/article.cfm/3329196?f=archives&origin=archive

Oxley, M. G. (2004, July 22). *Opening statement of Chairman Michael G. Oxley, Committee on Financial Services.* Retrieved August 14, 2004, from

http://financialservices.house.gov/media/pdf/072204.pdf

Pare, M. (2005, May 3). Tennessee legislator wants Sarbanes-Oxley Act reworked. *Chattanooga Times/Free Press.* Retrieved May 4, 2005, from

http://www.highbeam.com/library/doc3.asp?ctrlInfo=Round91%3AProd%3ADOC%3APrint&DOCID=1G1:132073627&print=yes

Parvaz, D. (2005). Corporate ethics: Business' big boys haven't cornered the market on bad. *Seattle Post-Intelligencer.* Retrieved September 13, 2005 from

http://www.highbeam.com/library/doc3asp?DOCID=1G1:111578889&alert_topic=SARBANES-OXLEY+ACT+OF+2002.

Paul, P.C. (2005, June 7). Small banks check into going private: Requirements of

    Sarbanes-Oxley Act cited. *The Atlanta Journal and Constitution*. Retrieved June

    8, 2005 from

    http://www.highbeam.com/library/doc3.asp?DOCID=1P1:109700190&ctrlInfo=

    Round10%3AProd%3ADOC%3APrint&print=yes

Pellet, J. (2003, December). *Audit angst*. Retrieved June 20, 2004, from

    http://articles.findarticles.com/p/articles/mi_m0DTI/is_12_31/ai_111163603/print

Peters, A. L. (2002, March 19). *Prepared statement of Ms. Aulana L. Peters, member,*

    Public Oversight Board. Retrieved August 14, 2004, from

    http://banking.senate.gov/02_03hrg/031902/peters.htm

Pitt, H. L. (2002, March 21). *Prepared statement of the Honorable Harvey L. Pitt,*

    chairman, Securities and Exchange Commission. Retrieved August 14, 2004,

    from http://banking.senate.gov/02_03hrg/032102/pitt.htm

PricewaterhouseCoopers. (2003, July 23). *Senior executives less favorable on Sarbanes-*

    Oxley, PricewaterhouseCoopers finds. Retrieved April 15, 2004, from

    http://www.pwcglobal.com/extweb/ncpressrelease.nsf/docid/42447F8971FD81B8

    85256D6B006

Prism. (2004). *The Prism guide to interpreting statistical results*. Retrieved April 6, 2005,

    from

    http://www.graphpad.com/articles/interpret/Analyzing_two_groups/choos_anal_c

    omp_two.htm

PR Newswire Association LLC. (2005/1, March 8). *ICBA survey shows burdensome costs of Sarbox Section 404 compliance.* Retrieved March 10, 2005, from http://www.highbeam.com/library/doc3.asp?ctrlInfo=Round9j%3AProd%3ADOC%3Aprint&DOCID=1G1:129873469&print=yes

PR Newswire Association LLC. (2005/2, May 5). *Pioneer Oil and Gas announces "going private" transaction to reduce compliance costs.* Retrieved May 9, 2005, from http://www.gihgbeam.com/library/doc3.asp?ctrlInfo=Round91%3AProd%3ADOC%3APrint&DOCID=1G1:132158774&print= yes

Public Oversight Board. (2000, August 31). *The panel on audit effectiveness: Report and recommendations.* Retrieved September 26, 2004, from http://www.pobauditpanel.org/download.html

Public Company Accounting Oversight Board (PCAOB). (2003). *Our mission.* Retrieved June 10, 2005, from http://www.pacobus.org/.

Quigley, J. H. (2004, July 22). *James H. Quigley testimony.* Retrieved August 14, 2004, from http://financialservices.house.gov/media/pdf/072204jq/pdf

Ramos, M. (2003, January). *Auditors' responsibility for fraud detection.* Retrieved April 26, 2004, from http://www.aicpa.org/pubs/jofa/jan2003/ramos.htm

Reinstein, A., & Weirich, T. R. (2002, December). *Accounting issues at Enron.* Retrieved September 26, 2003, from http://www.nysscpa.org/cpajournal/2002/1202/features/f122002.htm

Reisinger, S. (2005, July). Learning to love SOX. *Corporate Counsel, 12,* 16-17.

Rezaee, Z. (2002). *Financial statement fraud: Prevention and detection.* New York: John Wiley & Sons, Inc.

Rezaee, Z. (2003). *Causes, consequences, and deterrence of financial statement fraud.* Retrieved May 20, 2004, from http://www.irc.unizh.ch/studium/veranstaltungen/SS04/hauptstudium/325_interna l_and_external_auditing/downloads/papers/23_Rezaee_2003.pdf

Richardson, J. (2005, February 1). Column: Law keeps tight leash on businesses. *University Wire.* Retrieved February 3, 2005, from http://www.highbeam.com/library/doc3asp?DOCID=1P1:1049921686&num=14 &ctrlInfo=Round17%3AProd%3ASR%3AResult&ao=&FreePremium=BOTH

Roper, B. (2002, March 13). *Testimony of Barbara Roper, Director of Investor Protection, Consumer Federation of America before the Financial Services Committee of the U.S. House of Representatives regarding H.R. 3763, "The Corporate and Auditing Accountability, Responsibility and Transparency Act."* Retrieved August 14, 2004, from http://financialservices.house.gov/media/pdf/031302br.pdf

Rossant, J. (2004). Up front: Over there: Who needs U.S. markets? *Business Week.* Retrieved February 13, 2004, from http://www.highbeam.com/library/doc3.asp?DOCID=1P1:90130965

Rossi III, J. D. (2002). *How Enron jumped the GAAP.* Retrieved October 4, 2003, from http://www.moravian.edu/news/magazine/spring02/enron1.htm

Ruder, D. S. (2002, February 12). *Prepared statement of the Honorable David S. Ruder, chairman, Securities and Exchange Commission, 1987-1989.* Retrieved August 14, 2004, from http://banking.senate.gov/02_02hrg/021202/ruder.htm

Salavei, K., & Moore, N. (2004, November 18). *Signals sent by financial statement restatements*. Retrieved August 26, 2005, from http://www.fma.org/Siena/Papers/340077.pdf#search='cost%20restatements'

Sarbanes, P. S. (2004 August 25). *Letter to Ms. Debbie L. Yabrof, CPA.* Washington, DC.

Scherer, R., & Francis, D. R. (2002, January 16). *Lessons of Enron: How could no one have seen it?* Retrieved August 18, 2004, from http://www.csmonitor.com/2002/0116/p1s1-usec.htm

Securities and Exchange Commission (SEC). (2000, January 10). *Final rule: Audit committee disclosure*. Retrieved January 25, 2005, from http://www.sec.gov/rules.final/34-42266.htm

Securities and Exchange Commission (SEC). (2002). *United States District Court, Southern District of Texas, Houston Division*. Retrieved October 5, 2003, from http://www.sec.gov/litigation/complaints/comp17692.htm

Securities and Exchange Commission (SEC). (2004/1, April 30). *Report on the administrative proceedings for the period October 1, 2003 through March 31, 2004*. Retrieved February 22, 2005, from http://www.sec.gov/news/studies/34-49635.htm

Securities and Exchange Commission (SEC). (2004/2, October 27). *Division of enforcement*. Retrieved February 22, 2005, from http://www.sec.gov/divisions/enforce.shtml

Securities and Exchange Commission (SEC). (2004/3, December 2). *Fair administration and governance of self-regulatory organizations; disclosure and regulatory reporting by self-regulatory organizations; recordkeeping requirements for self-regulatory organizations; ownership and voting limitations for members of self-regulatory organizations; ownership reporting requirements for members of self-regulatory organizations; listing and trading of affiliated securities by a self-regulatory organization.* Retrieved January 26, 2005, from http://www.sec.gov/rules/proposed/34-50699.htm

Securities and Exchange Commission (SEC). (2004/4). *Form 8-K.* Retrieved January 27, 2005, from http://www.sec.gov/about/forms/form8-K.pdf

Securities and Exchange Commission (SEC). (2004/5). *Form 10-K.* Retrieved January 27, 2005, from http://www.sec.gov/about/forms/form10-K.pdf

Securities and Exchange Commission (SEC). (2004/6). *Form 10-Q.* Retrieved January 27, 2005, from http://www.sec.gov/about/forms/form10-Q.pdf

Seidman, L. W. (2002, March 19). *Prepared statement of Mr. L. William Seidman, former chairman of the Federal Deposit Insurance Corporation and Resolution Trust Corporation.* Retrieved August 14, 2004, from http://banking.senate.gov/02_03hrg/031902/seidman.htm

Senate. (2002/1, July 8). *Public Company Accounting Reform and Investor Protection Act of 2002.* Retrieved August 5, 2004, from http://thomas.loc.gov/cgi-bin/query/C?r107:./temp/~r107NEbSoW

Senate. (2002/2, July 10). *Public Company Accounting Reform and Investor Protection Act of 2002.* Retrieved August 5, 2004, from http://thomas.loc.gov/cgi-bin/query/C?r107:./temp/~r107728jNA

Senate. (2002/3, July 10). *The need to enact accounting and corporate reforms.* Retrieved August 5, 2004, from http://thomas.loc.gov/cgi-bin/query/F?r107:9:./temp/~r107K9MZPp:e0:

Senate. (2002/4, July 11). *Investor confidence.* Retrieved August 5, 2004, from http://thomas.loc.gov/cgi-bin/query/C?r107:./temp/~r107nL9TLO

Senate. (2002/5, July 11). *Public Company Accounting Reform and Investor Protection Act of 2002.* Retrieved August 8, 2004, from http://thomas.loc.gov/cgi-bin/query/F?R107:30:./temp/~r107hfRerl:e20362:

Senate. (2002/6, July 12). *Public Company Accounting and Investor Protection Act of 2002.* Retrieved August 5, 2004, from http://thomas.loc.gov/cgi-bin/query/C?r107:./temp/~r107lMu5nl

Senate. (2002/7, July 15). *Public Company Accounting Reform and Investor Protection Act of 2002.* Retrieved August 8, 2004, from http://thomas.loc.gov/cgi-bin/query/C?r107:./temp/~r107DE3B9U

Senate. (2002/8, July 25). *Sarbanes-Oxley Act of 2002-conference report.* Retrieved August 5, 2004, from http://thomas.loc.gov/cgi-bin/query/C?r107:./temp/~r107WnXrcZ

SmartPros. (2004). *Investors believe SOX will protect their investments.* Retrieved April 7, 2004, from http://accounting.smartpros.com/x42316.xml

StatSoft, Inc. (2003). *Elementary concepts in statistics*. Retrieved February 16, 2005,

 from http://www.statsoft.com/textbook/esc.html

Sutton, M. H. (2002, February 26). *Prepared statement of Mr. Michael H. Sutton, chief*

 accountant, Securities and Exchange Commission, 1995-98. Retrieved August 14,

 2002, from http://banking.senate.gov/02_02hrg/022602/sutton.htm

Tapscott, D., & Ticoll, D. (2003). *The naked corporation: How the age of transparency*

 will revolutionize business. New York: Simon & Schuster, Inc.

Teslik, S. (2002, March 20). *Prepared statement of Ms. Sarah Teslik, executive director,*

 Council of Institutional Investors. Retrieved August 14, 2004, from

 http://banking.senate.gov/02_03hrg/032002/teslik.htm

The Corporate Library. (2002). *Spotlight topic: Special purpose entities (SPEs)*.

 Retrieved October 5, 2003, from

 http://www.thecorporatelibrary.com/spotlight/accounting/SPEs.html

The Free Dictionary. (2005). Whistleblower. Retrieved January 25, 2005 from

 http://www.thefreedictionary.com/whistleblower

The Institute of Internal Auditors. (2005). *Definition of internal auditing*. Retrieved

 January 25, 2005, from

 http://www.theiia.org/iia/index.cfm?act=content.print&doc_id=123

Trumka, R. L. (2004, July 22). *Statement for the record of Richard L. Trumka, secretary-*

 treasurer, American Federation of Labor and Congress of Industrial

 Organizations before the Financial Serivces Committee, United States House of

 Representatives. Retrieved August 14, 2004, from

 http://financialservices.house.gov/media/pdf/072204rt.pdf

Turner, L. E. (2002, February 26). *Prepared statement of Mr. Lynn E. Turner, chief accountant, Securities and Exchange Commission, 1998-2001.* Retrieved August 14, 2002, from http://banking.senate.gov/02_02hrg/022602/turner.htm

Ulick, J. (2002, June 26). *WorldCom's financial bomb.* Retrieved August 26, 2005, from http://money.cnn.com/2002/06/25/news/worldcom/index.htm

United Press International. (2004). *New accounting rules hurt profitability.* Retrieved February 12, 2004, from

http://www.highbeam.com/library/doc3asp?DOCID=1P1:90955754

Virginia University. (2003). Assumptions of a t-test. Retrieved April 5, 2005, from http://www.evsc.virginia.edu/~jhp7e/EVSC503/slides/lec7/tsld013.htm

Volcker, P. (2002, February 14). *Prepared statement of the Honorable Paul Volcker, chairman of the Trustees of the International Accounting Standards Board; chairman of Arthur Andersen's Independent Oversight Board; and former chairman, Board of Governors of the Federal Reserve System.* Retrieved August 14, 2004, from http://banking.senate.gov/02_02hrg/021402/volcker.htm

Walker, D. M. (2002, March 5). *Protecting the public interest: Selected governance, regulatory oversight, auditing, accounting, and financial reporting issues.* Retrieved August 14, 2004, from http://gao.gov/new.items/d02483t.pdf

Walker, T. (2005, July 26). Metaphors about market carry weight. *The Atlanta Journal and Constitution.* Retrieved July 29, 2005 from http://www.highbeam.com/library/doc3.asp?DOCID=1P1:111453246&alert_topic=SARBANES-OXLEY+ACT+OF+2002

Walters, P. (2005, May 15). Greenspan urges Wharton grads to be honest. *AP Online*.

    Retrieved May 16, 2005 from

    http://www.highbeam.com/library/doc3.asp?ctrlInfo=Round91%3AProd%3aDO

    C%3aPrint&DOCID=1P1:108748958&print=yes

Whitehead, J. C. (2002, March 19). *Prepared statement of Mr. John C. Whitehead,*

    former co-chairman of Goldman Sachs & Co., former Deputy Secretary of State.

    Retrieved August 14, 2004, from

    http://banking.senate.gov/02_03hrg/031902/whithead.htm

Williams, H. M. (2002, February 12). *Prepared statement of the Honorable Harold M.*

    Williams, chairman, Securities and Exchange Commission, 1977-1981. Retrieved

    August 14, 2004, from http://banking.senate.gov/02_02hrg/021202/williams.htm

Zhang, I.X. (2003, February). *Economic Consequences of the Sarbanes-Oxley Act of*

    2002. Retrieved January 7, 2006 from

    http://w4.stern.nyu.edu/accounting/docs/speaker_papers/Spring2005/Zhang_Ivy_

    Economic_Consequences_of_S_O.pdf#search='SarbanesOxley20%Dissertation'

APPENDIX A

SOX Summary

SOX Summary (One Hundred Seventh Congress of the United States of America, 2002)

Section

1   Short Title; Table of Contents
2   Definitions
3   Commission Rules and Enforcement

TITLE I - PUBLIC COMPANY ACCOUNTING OVERSIGHT BOARD

101   Establishment; Administrative Provisions (Board Duties and Membership)

(a) Public Company Accounting Oversight Board (Board)
  Oversee audit of public companies.

(b) Not an agency or establishment of US Government - nonprofit agency

(c) Register public accounting firms, establish auditing standards, inspect public accounting firms, conduct investigations and disciplinary proceedings and impose sanctions against public accounting firms, enforce compliance with SOX.

(e) 5 member Board, with only 2 CPAs. Full time position.

(h) Submit annual report to SEC, who transmits copies to Senate Banking and House Finance Committees.

102   Registration With the Board

(a) Mandatory registration for public accounting firms auditing public companies.

(d) Registered public accounting firm submit annual report to Board and more frequently as requested.

(f) Registration fee and annual fees collected from each registered public accounting firm to recover costs of processing and reviewing applications and annual reports.

103   Auditing, QC, and Independence Standards and Rules

(a) Board establish standards proposed by one or more professional groups of accountants.

(2) Registered public accounting firm shall keep audit work papers for seven years; have concurring or second partner review; describe scope of auditor's testing of IC and results in audit report; requirements of registered public accounting firms to monitor pro ethics and independence, consultation, hiring, professional development, and advancement of personnel, acceptance and continuation of engagements.

(4) Board shall convene and consult expert advisory groups as appropriate and necessary.

104   Inspections of Registered Public Accounting Firms

(b) Inspect firms annually that provide audit reports for greater than100 issuers, or once every 3 yrs for others.

105   Investigations and Disciplinary Proceedings

(b)(3) If registered accounting firm or associated person refuses to cooperate with investigation, subject to suspension from firm, or suspension or revocation of registration, as well as fines, etcetera.

(4) Investigation may be referred to SEC.

(5) Documents used in investigations are confidential, but are available to SEC and other government agencies.

(c)(2) Hearings shall not be public.

(d) Sanctions to be reported to SEC, appropriate state agency, and the public.

106   Foreign Public Accounting Firms

(a) Any foreign public accounting firm providing audit report for issuer shall be subject to SOX.

(c) SEC and Board may exempt a foreign public accounting firm.

107   Commission Oversight of the Board

(a) SEC has oversight and enforcement authority over Board.

(b) No rule of Board becomes effective without prior approval of SEC.

(c) Review by SEC of final disciplinary sanctions imposed by Board, and SEC may modify sanctions.

(d) SEC may relieve Board of any responsibility, or censure or impose limitations upon Board.

(3) May also remove from office or censure any member of Board.

108   Accounting Standards

(a) Amendment to Securities Act of 1933

SEC recognize as GAAP accounting principles established by private standard setting body, funded as in Section 109, acting in public interest.

(d) SEC shall conduct study on adoption by US of principles-based accounting system.

109   Funding

(b) Board shall establish annual budget.

(c) Funds from accounting support fees and collection of monetary penalties.

(f) Fees shall not exceed recoverable budget expenses for the year.

TITLE II - AUDITOR INDEPENDENCE

201   Services Outside the Scope of Practice of Auditors (Prohibited Activities)

(a) Amends Securities Exchange Act of 1934 (1934 Act) - Unlawful for public accounting firm to perform for client:

(1) Bookkeeping

(2) Financial information system design and implementation

(3) Appraisal or valuation services, fairness opinions, or contribution-in-kind reports

(4) Actuarial services

(5) Internal audit outsourcing services

(6) Management functions or human resources

(7) Broker or dealer, investment adviser, or investment banking services

(8) Legal services and expert services unrelated to the audit

(9) Any other service that Board determines, by regulation, is impermissible

Audit committee must preapprove any other non-audit services, including taxes.

(b) Board has exemption authority.

202   Preapproval Requirements

Amends Section 10A of 1934 Act.

All auditing and non-audit services provided to an issuer by the auditor of the issuer shall be preapproved by the audit committee of the issuer.

The preapproval requirement is waived if (a) the aggregate amount of all such non-audit services are not more than five percent of total amount paid to auditor, (b) the services were not recognized by the issuer to be non-audit services at the time of the engagement, and (c) such audit services are promptly brought to the attention of the audit committee and approved prior to the end of the engagement.

203   Audit Partner Rotation

Amends Section 10A of 1934 Act.

Unlawful for registered public accounting firm to provide services if lead audit partner or audit partner responsible for reviewing audit has performed services for that issuer in each of the five previous years of that issuer.

204   Audit Reports to Audit Committees

Amends Section 10A of 1934 Act.

Registered public accounting firm shall report to issuer's audit committee:

(1) All critical accounting policies and practices to be used

(2) Alternative treatments of financial information within GAAP

(3) Other material written communications between firm and management of issuer

205   Conforming Amendments

(a) Amends Section 3(a) of 1934 Act for definition of audit committee and registered public accounting firm.

(b) Amends 1934 Act by replacing "independent public accountant" with "registered public accounting firm."

206   Conflicts of Interest

Amends 1934 Act.

Unlawful for registered public accounting firm to provide services if CEO, CFO, controller, CAO or any person in equivalent position was employed by firm and participated in audit during one-year period preceding date of initiation of audit.

207   Study of Mandatory Rotation of Registered Public Accountants

(a) Comptroller General of US will study effects of requiring mandatory rotation of registered public accounting firms.

(b) Comptroller General shall submit report on results of study to Senate Banking Committee and House Finance Committee.

208   Commission Authority

(b) Unlawful for any registered public accounting firm to issue audit report if performed any prohibited services.

209   Consideration by Appropriate State Regulatory Authorities

Standards applied by Board under SOX shall not be presumed to be applicable for purposes of this section for small and medium sized nonregistered public accounting firms.

TITLE III - CORPORATE RESPONSIBILITY

301   Public Company Audit Committees

Audit committee directly responsible for appointment, compensation, and oversight of work of any registered public accounting firm employed by issuer, and registered public accounting firm shall report directly to the audit committee.

Audit committee members shall be independent. SEC has exemption authority on this.

Audit committee shall have procedures to handle complaints received by issuer concerning accounting, internal accounting controls, or auditing matters.

Audit committee shall have procedures for confidential, anonymous submission of employees concerning questionable accounting or auditing matters.

Audit committee has authority to engage independent counsel or other advisers.

Issuer to pay for registered public accounting firm and any outside advisers or counsel.

302   Corporate Responsibility for Financial Reports

(a) CEO and CFO certify in annual or quarterly reports filed that:

(1) Signing officer has reviewed report.

(2) Based on officer's knowledge, report not contain any untrue statement of material fact or omit to state material fact that would make

statements misleading.

(3) Statements and other financial information fairly present in all material respects the financial condition and results of operations of issuer for periods presented.

(4) The signing officers are responsible for internal control (IC), have evaluated their effectiveness, and include conclusions in the report.

(5) Signing officers have disclosed to auditors and audit committee any weaknesses in IC and any known fraud.

(6) Signing officers have indicated in report any changes to IC.

(c) Shall take effect not later than 30 days after enactment of act.

303   Improper Influence on Conduct of Audits

(a) Unlawful for any officer or director of issuer or agent thereof, to take any fraudulent action to influence, coerce, manipulate, or mislead independent or public accountant.

(b) SEC has enforcement authority.

(d) SEC propose rules or regulations for section within 90 days after enactment of SOX, and issue final rules or regulations within 270 days after enactment of SOX.

304   Forfeiture of Certain Bonuses and Profits

(a) If restatement of financials occurs due to material noncompliance or misconduct, the CEO and CFO shall reimburse issuer for bonuses or other incentives received within 12 months of first filing statement, as well as profits realized from sale of issuer securities within same 12-month period.

(b) SEC has exemption authority.

305   Officer and Director Bars and Penalties (Equitable Relief)

(a) Amend Securities Exchange Act of 1933 (1933 Act) and 1934 Act by striking "substantial unfitness" and inserting "unfitness."

(b) Amend Section 21(d) of 1934 Act to give equitable relief for benefit of investors.

306   Insider Trades During Pension Fund Blackout Periods

(a) Unlawful for any director or executive officer of issuer to purchase, sell, or otherwise acquire or transfer any equity security of issuer during any blackout period if such director or officer acquires such equity security in connection with his or her services of employment as director or officer.

(b) Provisions of this section take effect 180 days after date of enactment of SOX.

307   Rules of Professional Responsibility for Attorneys

Not later than 180 days after enactment of SOX, SEC shall issue rules setting forth minimum standards of professional conduct for attorneys appearing and practicing before the SEC.

308 Fair Funds for Investors
  (a) Disgorgement monies required by any judicial or administrative action brought by SEC under securities laws shall become part of disgorgement fund for benefit of victims of violation.
  (b) Donations can be accepted into the fund.

TITLE IV - ENHANCED FINANCIAL DISCLOSURES
401 Disclosures in Periodic Reports
  (a) Amends Section 13 of 1934 Act - Financial reports filed with SEC shall reflect all material correcting adjustments from auditors, and SEC will issue final rules within 180 days after enactment of SOX requiring disclosure of all material off-balance sheet transactions.
  (b) Within 180 days after enactment of SOX, SEC shall issue final rules requiring pro forma statements that do not contain any untrue material facts or omit material facts, and reconciles with financial condition and results of operations of issuer.
  (c) Within one year of effective date of adoption of off-balance sheet disclosure rules, SEC shall complete study of extent of such transactions and if, per GAAP, they are transparent to investors. SEC shall submit report of study to the President, Senate Banking and House Finance Committees.
402 Enhanced Conflict of Interest Provisions
  (a) Amends Section 13 of 1934 Act - Prohibits personal loans or extension of credit to executives unless within ordinary course of business of issuer.
403 Disclosures of Transactions Involving Management and Principal Stockholders
  (a) Amends Section 16 of 1934 Act.
  Owner of greater than ten percent of any class of equity security must file required statements at time of registration of such security on a national exchange, within ten days after becoming owner, director, or officer. If change in ownership, must file by end of second business day following day of transaction.
  (b) Effective 30 days after enactment of SOX.
404 Management Assessment of Internal Controls
  (a) SEC proscribe rules requiring annual report to contain IC report, which states management responsibility to establish and maintain adequate IC structure and procedures, and contain assessment of effectiveness of IC.
  (b) Registered public accounting firm shall attest to and report on assessment of IC made by management of issuer, and include in audit report.
405 Exemption

Not apply to any investment company registered under section 8 of Investment Company Act of 1940.

406 Code of Ethics for Senior Financial Officers
(a) SEC shall issue rules to require each issuer to disclose adoption of code of ethics for senior financial officers, and if not, why not.
(b) SEC to revise rules to require immediate disclosure of any changes in code of ethics for senior financial officers.
(d) SEC shall propose such rules within 90 days after enactment of SOX, and issue final rules within 180 days of enactment of SOX.

407 Disclosure of Audit Committee Financial Expert
(a) SEC shall issue rules to require each issuer to disclose whether or not, and if not why not, audit committee is comprised of at least one financial expert.
(c) SEC shall propose rules within 90 days after enactment of SOX, and issue final rules within 180 days after enactment of SOX.

408 Enhanced Review of Periodic Disclosures by Issuers
(a) SEC shall review disclosures and financial statements of issuers on a regular and systematic basis for protection of investors.
(b) To schedule reviews, SEC will consider any material restatements made; significant volatility in stock price; issuers with largest market capitalization; emerging companies with disparities in price to earnings ratios; issuers whose operations significantly affect any material sector of economy; and any other factors SEC may consider relevant.
(c) Issuer will be reviewed at least every three years.

409 Real Time Issuer Disclosures
Amends Section 13 of 1934 Act, saying issuers must disclose to public on rapid and current basis additional information concerning material changes in financial condition or operations of issuer. May include trend and qualitative information and graphic presentations, as SEC determines.

TITLE V - ANALYST CONFLICTS OF INTEREST
501 Treatment of Securities Analysts by Registered Securities Associations and National Securities Exchanges
(a) Amends 1934 Act by adding Section 15D.
(a) Registered securities association or national securities exchange shall have adopted, within one year of enactment of this section, rules designed to address conflicts of interest with securities analysts.
(b) Within one year of enactment of this section, registered securities association or national securities exchange shall have adopted rules to require securities analysts, brokers, and dealers to disclose conflicts of interest.

TITLE VI - COMMISSION RESOURCES AND AUTHORITY

601 SEC Resources and Authority
Amends Section 35 of 1934 Act. Allocates additional funds to SEC.

602 Appearance and Practice Before the Commission
Amends 1934 Act by inserting Section 4C.
Commission may censure any person, or deny, temporarily or permanently, to any person the privilege of appearing or practicing before SEC if person lacking qualifications to represent others, lacking in character or integrity, or violated securities laws.

603 Federal Court Authority to Impose Penny Stock Bars
(a) Amends Section 21(d) of 1934 Act. Court may prohibit person from participating in an offering of penny stock, conditionally or unconditionally, permanently, or court shall determine time.
(b) Amends Section 20 of 1933 Act. Same as (a).

604 Qualifications of Associated Persons of Brokers and Dealers
(a) Amends Section 15(b)(4) of 1934 Act. SEC can bar or suspend the right of a person from being associated with a broker or dealer.
(b) Amends Section 203(e) of Investment Advisers Act of 1940. Same as (a).

TITLE VII - STUDIES AND REPORTS

701 GAO Study and Report Regarding Consolidation of Public Accounting Firms
(a) Comptroller General of U.S. conduct study as to consolidation of public accounting firms since 1989 and consequent reduction in number of qualified firms. Problems, if any, because of higher costs, lower quality of services, impairment of auditor independence, and lack of choice.
(b) Comptroller General shall consult with SEC, regulatory agencies, DOJ, any other public or private sector organization deemed appropriate.
(c) Report to be submitted within one year of enactment of SOX, to Senate Banking Committee and House Finance Committee.

702 Commission Study and Report Regarding Credit Rating Agencies
(a) SEC to conduct study of role and function of credit rating agencies in operation of securities market.
(b) SEC shall submit report to President, and Senate Banking and House Finance Committees no later than 180 days after date of enactment of SOX.

703 Study and Report on Violators and Violations
(a) SEC to conduct study to determine number of securities professionals who have aided and abetted in violation of securities laws, or have been

158

primary violators; description of these violations; and disgorgement, restitution, or fines or payments assessed from these violators.

(b) Report shall be submitted to Senate Banking Committee and House Finance Committee no later than 6 months after enactment of SOX.

704   Study of Enforcement Actions

(a) SEC to review and analyze enforcement actions by SEC involving violations of reporting requirements imposed under securities laws, and restatements, over 5 year period preceding enactment of SOX.

(b) SEC shall submit report to Senate Banking and House Finance Committees no later than 180 days after enactment of SOX. Use findings to revise rules and regulations.

705   Study of Investment Banks

(a) Comptroller General of U.S. shall conduct study as to whether investment banks and financial advisers assisted public companies in manipulating their earnings and obfuscating their true financial condition.

(b) Report shall be submitted to Congress not later than 180 days after date of enactment of SOX.

TITLE VIII - CORPORATE AND CRIMINAL FRAUD ACCOUNTABILITY

801   Short Title

802   Criminal Penalties for Altering Documents

(a) Destruction, alteration, or falsification of records in Federal investigations and bankruptcy shall be fined, or imprisoned not more than 20 years, or both. Auditor shall maintain all audit or review workpapers for five years from end of the fiscal period in which audit or review was concluded. Destruction of corporate audit records shall lead to fine, or imprisonment for not more than 10 years, or both.

803   Debts Nondischargeable if Incurred in Violation of Securities Fraud Laws

804   Statute of Limitations for Securities Fraud

(a) Private right of action for securities laws may be brought not later than the earlier of two years after the discovery of facts constituting violation, or five years after such violation.

(b) Shall apply to all proceedings addressed by this section that are commenced on or after date of enactment of SOX.

805   Review of Federal Sentencing Guidelines for Obstruction of Justice and Extensive Criminal Fraud

(a) Guidelines for offense levels and sentencing enhancements for violations are sufficient to deter and punish obstruction of justice, extensive criminal fraud, and organizational criminal misconduct.

(b) To be enacted as soon as practicable, or not later than 180 days after date of enactment of SOX.

806   Protection for Employees of Publicly Traded Companies Who Provide Evidence of Fraud

(a) Protection of whistleblowers - No public company or agent of such company may discharge, demote, suspend, threaten, harass, or in any other manner discriminate against a whistleblower employee.

(b) Any person who alleges discharge or other discrimination in violation of (a) may seek relief with the Secretary of Labor.

(c) Employee prevailing shall be entitled to all relief necessary to make employee whole.

807   Criminal Penalties for Defrauding Shareholders of Publicly Traded Companies

If anyone knowingly executes or attempts to execute a scheme or artifice of securities fraud shall be fined, or imprisoned not more than 25 years, or both.

TITLE IX - WHITE-COLLAR CRIME PENALTY ENHANCEMENTS

901   Short Title

902   Attempts and Conspiracies to Commit Criminal Fraud Offenses

Any person who attempts or conspires to commit any offense under this chapter shall be subject to the same penalties as those prescribed for the offense.

903   Criminal Penalties for Mail and Wire Fraud

(a) Mail fraud - 20 years instead of five years.

(b) Wire fraud - 20 years instead of five years.

904   Criminal Penalties for Violations of the Employee Retirement Income Security Act of 1974

Amend Section 501 of ERISA:

Instead of $5,000, insert $100,000

Instead of one year, insert 10 years

Instead of $100,000, insert $500,000

905   Amendment to Sentencing Guidelines Relating to Certain White-Collar Offenses

(b) U.S. Sentencing Commission shall ensure that sentencing guidelines and policy statements reflect the serious nature of offenses in SOX, and are sufficient to deter and punish these offenses and are adequate in view of statutory increases in penalties contained in SOX.

(c) Guidelines or amendments should be done as soon as practicable, or not later than 180 days after the enactment of SOX.

906   Corporate Responsibility for Financial Reports

Whoever certifies financial statements knowing that the periodic report accompanying the statement does not comport with all the requirements set forth shall be fined not more than $1,000,000, or imprisoned more than 10 years, or both.

Whoever willfully certifies any statement knowing that the periodic report accompanying the statement does not comport with all the requirements set forth shall be fined not more than $5,000,000, or imprisoned more than 20 years, or both.

TITLE X - CORPORATE TAX RETURNS

1001   Sense of the Senate Regarding the Signing of Corporate Tax Returns by CEOs

CEO should sign the Federal income tax return of a corporation.

TITLE XI - CORPORATE FRAUD AND ACCOUNTABILITY

1101   Short Title

1102   Tampering With a Record or Otherwise Impeding an Official Proceeding

Whoever alters, destroys, mutilates, or conceals a record, document, or other object, or attempts to do so, with the intent to impair object's integrity or availability for use in an official proceeding; or otherwise obstructs, influences, or impedes any official proceeding, or attempts to do so; shall be fined, or imprisoned not more than 20 years, or both.

1103   Temporary Freeze Authority for the SEC

(a) SEC may escrow extraordinary payments in an interest-bearing account for 45 days. Extensions may be given by the court for good cause.

1104   Amendment to the Federal Sentencing Guidelines

(a) U.S. Sentencing Commission is to promptly review sentencing guidelines applicable to securities, accounting fraud, and related offenses, and submit to Congress an explanation of actions taken and additional policy recommendations.

(b) U.S. Sentencing Commission shall ensure that sentencing guidelines and policy statements reflect the serious nature of offenses in SOX, and are sufficient to deter and punish these offenses and are adequate in view of statutory increases in penalties contained in SOX, especially as they relate to obstruction of justice where documents or other physical evidence is actually destroyed or fabricated.

(c) Shall be enacted as soon as practicable, and not later than 180 days after the date of enactment of SOX.

1105   Authority of SEC to Prohibit Persons from Serving as Officers or Directors

(a) Amends Section 21C of 1934 Act.

In cease-and-desist proceeding, SEC may issue order to prohibit, conditionally or unconditionally, permanently or temporarily, any person who has violated section 10(b) rules or regulations, from acting as officer or director of any issuer.

(b) Also amends Section 8A of 1933 Act in same way.

1106   Increased Criminal Penalties Under Securities Exchange Act of 1934
Amends Section 32(a) of 1934 Act.

Instead of $1,000,000 or imprisoned not more than 10 years, insert $5,000,000 or imprisoned not more than 20 years.

Instead of $2,500,000 insert $25,000,000

1107   Retaliation Against Informants

Whoever knowingly, with intent to retaliate, takes any action harmful to any person, including interference with lawful employment or livelihood of any person, for providing to law enforcement officer any truthful information relating to commission or possible commission of any Federal offense, shall be fined or imprisoned not more than 10 years, or both.

APPENDIX B

SEC Enforcement Statistics With
Formulas

SEC Enforcement Statistics With Formulas

Federal Court Actions

2005-2006		2004-2005		2003-2004		2002-2003		2001-2002		2000-2001		1999-2000	
10/05	39	10/04	36	10/03	58	10/02	65	10/01	49	10/00	44	10/99	24
11/05	30	11/04	36	11/03	40	11/02	45	11/01	35	11/00	27	11/99	28
12/05	38	12/04	32	12/03	49	12/02	44	12/01	41	12/00	33	12/99	24
		1/05	39	1/04	34	1/03	48	1/02	58	1/01	39	1/00	23
		2/05	47	2/04	40	2/03	49	2/02	38	2/01	35	2/00	41
		3/05	60	3/04	49	3/03	49	3/02	61	3/01	28	3/00	38
		4/05	46	4/04	37	4/03	64	4/02	49	4/01	31	4/00	32
		5/05	31	5/04	41	5/03	41	5/02	42	5/01	41	5/00	46
		6/05	50	6/04	44	6/03	44	6/02	55	6/01	37	6/00	40
		7/05	27	7/04	42	7/03	60	7/02	52	7/01	25	7/00	24
		8/05	36	8/04	47	8/03	51	8/02	60	8/01	30	8/00	34
		9/05	57	9/04	53	9/03	64	9/02	51	9/01	54	9/00	68
Totals	107		497		534		624		591		424		422

Formulas	8/02-9/02 (6 month result)	$(60+51)/(49+42+55+52+60+51) = 35.92\%$
	8/02-9/02 (12 month result)	$(60+51)/591 = 18.78\%$
	8/02-12/02	$(60+51+65+45+44)/(591-49-35-41+65+45+44) = 42.74\%$

Admininstrative Law Judges (ALJ) Initial Decisions & Orders

2005-2006		2004-2005		2003-2004		2002-2003		2001-2002		2000-2001		1999-2000	
10/05	1	10/04	5	10/03	2	10/02	0	10/01	1	10/00	1	10/99	2
11/05	2	11/04	1	11/03	2	11/02	1	11/01	1	11/00	3	11/99	0
12/05	3	12/04	2	12/03	1	12/02	3	12/01	2	12/00	2	12/99	?
		1/05	4	1/04	3	1/03	1	1/02	1	1/01	2	1/00	5
		2/05	8	2/04	1	2/03	4	2/02	2	2/01	0	2/00	1
		3/05	2	3/04	2	3/03	1	3/02	1	3/01	2	3/00	1
		4/05	4	4/04	3	4/03	0	4/02	1	4/01	0	4/00	1
		5/05	4	5/04	2	5/03	3	5/02	2	5/01	2	5/00	3
		6/05	5	6/04	1	6/03	3	6/02	2	6/01	1	6/00	2
		7/05	3	7/04	2	7/03	2	7/02	3	7/01	1	7/00	2
		8/05	1	8/04	1	8/03	0	8/02	4	8/01	2	8/00	1
		9/05	4	9/04	6	9/03	4	9/02	3	9/01	5	9/00	1
Totals	6	Totals	43		26		22		23		21		21

Formulas	8/02-9/02 (6 month result)	$(4+3)/(1+2+2+3+4+3) = 46.67\%$
	8/02-9/02 (12 month result)	$(3+4)/23 = 30.43\%$
	8/02-12/02	$(3+4+0+1+3)/(23-1-1-2+0+1+3) = 47.83\%$

Administrative Proceedings

2005-2006		2004-2005		2003-2004		2002-2003		2001-2002		2000-2001		1999-2000	
10/05	46	10/04	51	10/03	39	10/02	25	10/01	19	10/00	19	10/99	20
11/05	29	11/04	40	11/03	26	11/02	38	11/01	22	11/00	17	11/99	30
12/05	44	12/04	53	12/03	26	12/02	52	12/01	27	12/00	39	12/99	22
		1/05	36	1/04	17	1/03	35	1/02	27	1/01	19	1/00	6
		2/05	38	2/04	43	2/03	32	2/02	23	2/01	25	2/00	25
		3/05	50	3/04	37	3/03	36	3/02	42	3/01	25	3/00	22
		4/05	69	4/04	25	4/03	31	4/02	33	4/01	17	4/00	32
		5/05	26	5/04	42	5/03	48	5/02	17	5/01	37	5/00	20
		6/05	47	6/04	32	6/03	32	6/02	35	6/01	44	6/00	39
		7/05	40	7/04	53	7/03	37	7/02	45	7/01	23	7/00	16
		8/05	50	8/04	73	8/03	47	8/02	27	8/01	21	8/00	20
		9/05	57	9/04	75	9/03	59	9/02	30	9/01	51	9/00	75
Totals	119	Totals	557		488		472		347		337		327

Formulas   8/02-9/02 (6 month result) $(27+30)/(33+17+35+45+27+30) = 30.48\%$

8/02-9/02 (12 month result) $(27+30)/347 = 16.43\%$

8/02-12/02 $(27+30+25+38+52)/(347-19-22-27+25+38+52) = 43.65\%$

Commission Opinions

2005-2006		2004-2005		2003-2004		2002-2003		2001-2002		2000-2001		1999-2000	
10/05	7	10/04	4	10/03	7	10/02	5	10/01	6	10/00	4	10/99	2
11/05	1	11/04	8	11/03	3	11/02	1	11/01	1	11/00	4	11/99	2
12/05	4	12/04	3	12/03	10	12/02	0	12/01	1	12/00	2	12/99	1
		1/05	2	1/04	2	1/03	3	1/02	3	1/01	5	1/00	3
		2/05	4	2/04	5	2/03	2	2/02	3	2/01	3	2/00	0
		3/05	1	3/04	3	3/03	12	3/02	1	3/01	1	3/00	1
		4/05	5	4/04	2	4/03	2	4/02	6	4/01	3	4/00	0
		5/05	2	5/04	2	5/03	3	5/02	3	5/01	5	5/00	2
		6/05	5	6/04	4	6/03	4	6/02	1	6/01	0	6/00	0
		7/05	3	7/04	6	7/03	10	7/02	2	7/01	2	7/00	1
		8/05	1	8/04	2	8/03	9	8/02	3	8/01	1	8/00	1
		9/05	1	9/04	6	9/03	5	9/02	1	9/01	0	9/00	3
Totals	12	Totals	39		52		56		31		30		16

Formulas

8/02-9/02 (6 month result) $(3+1)/(6+3+1+2+3+1) = 25.00\%$

8/02-9/02 (12 month result) $(3+1)/31 = 12.9\%$

8/02-12/02 $(3+1+5+1+0)/(31-6-1-1+5+1+0) = 34.48\%$

Trading Suspensions

2005-2006		2004-2005		2003-2004		2002-2003		2001-2002		2000-2001		1999-2000	
10/05	0	10/04	1	10/03	0	10/02	1	10/01	0	10/00	0	10/99	1
11/05	2	11/04	0	11/03	0	11/02	3	11/01	1	11/00	0	11/99	0
12/05	0	12/04	4	12/03	0	12/02	1	12/01	0	12/00	1	12/99	0
		1/05	2	1/04	0	1/03	2	1/02	3	1/01	0	1/00	0
		2/05	4	2/04	0	2/03	1	2/02	1	2/01	0	2/00	2
		3/05	2	3/04	3	3/03	2	3/02	1	3/01	1	3/00	3
		4/05	4	4/04	3	4/03	0	4/02	3	4/01	0	4/00	0
		5/05	2	5/04	0	5/03	1	5/02	1	5/01	0	5/00	1
		6/05	2	6/04	1	6/03	0	6/02	0	6/01	0	6/00	3
		7/05	7	7/04	0	7/03	1	7/02	1	7/01	0	7/00	1
		8/05	5	8/04	0	8/03	1	8/02	0	8/01	0	8/00	0
		9/05	1	9/04	1	9/03	0	9/02	0	9/01	0	9/00	0
Totals	2		34		8		13		11		2		11

Formulas	8/02-9/02 (6 month result)		$(0+0)/(3+1+0+1+0+0) = 0.00\%$
	8/02-9/02 (12 month result)		$(0+0)/11 = 0.00\%$
	8/02-12/02		$(0+0+1+3+1)/(11-0-1-0+1+3+1) = 33.33\%$

Formula Percentage Results

8/02-9/02 (6 month result) Percentage of the fiscal year October through September

Federal Court Actions	35.92%
Administrative Proceedings	30.48%
Commission Opinions	25.00%
Average	30.47%

Note: The highest and lowest percentages from the categories (46.67% from ALJ Initial Decisions & Orders, from Trading Suspensions) were eliminated so as not to skew the average.

8/02-9/02 (12 month result) Percentage of the fiscal year October through September

Federal Court Actions	18.78%
Administrative Proceedings	16.43%
Commission Opinions	12.90%
Average	16.04%

Note: The highest and lowest percentages from the categories (30.43% from ALJ Initial Decisions & Orders, and 0.00% from Trading Suspensions) were eliminated so as not to skew the average.

8/02-12/02 Percentage of the calendar year

Federal Court Actions	42.74%
Administrative Proceedings	43.65%
Commission Opinions	34.48%
Average	40.29%

Note: The highest and lowest percentages from the categories (47.83% from ALJ Initial Decisions & Orders, and 33.33% from Trading Suspensions) were eliminated so as not to skew the average.

APPENDIX C

CFTF Reports

	Total SEC Enforcement Actions Filed	SEC Financial Fraud & Issuer Reporting Actions Filed	SEC-Officer & Director Bars Sought
FY2004 (10/1/03-6/30/04)	378	81	113
FY 2004 annualized	504	108	151
FY 2003	679	199	170
FY 2002	598(a)	163(b)	126(c)
FY 2001	484	112	51
FY 2000	503	103	58
8/02-9/02	(a) (598x16.04%)/2	(b) (163x16.04%)/2	(c) (126x16.04%)/2
	x 12 = 575.52	x 12 = 156.90	x 12 = 121.26
10/01-7/02	(598x83.96%)/10	(163x83.96%)/10	(126x83.96%)/10
	x 120 = 602.50	x 120 = 164.22	x 120 =126.95

	SEC-Temporary Restraining Orders Filed	SEC-Asset Freezes	SEC-Subpoena Enforcement Proceedings
FY 2004 (10/1/03-6/30/04)	27	36	7
FY 2004 annualized	36	48	9
FY 2003	35	39	12
FY 2002	48(d)	63(e)	19(f)
FY 2001	31	43	15
FY 2000	33	56	8
8/02-9/02	(d) (48x16.04%)/2 x 12 = 46.20	(e) (63x16.04%)/2 x 12 = 60.66	(f) (19x16.04%)/2 x 12 = 18.30
10/01-7/02	(48x83.96%)/10 x 120 = 48.36	(63x83.96%)/10 x 120 = 63.47	(19x83.96%)/10 x 120 = 19.14

APPENDIX D

Huron Consulting Group - Financial Statement
Restatements

Huron Consulting Group - Financial Statement Restatements

	Restatements by Year Filed	Audited 10K Restatements by Year Filed	Audited 10Q Restatements by Year Filed
2004	414	253	161
2003	323	206	117
2002	330(a)	183(b)	147(c)
2001	270	140	130
2000	233	98	135
1999	216	116	100
8/02-12/02	(a) (330x40.29%)/5 x 12 = 319.10	(b) (183x40.29%)/5 x 12 = 176.95	(c) (147x40.29%)/5 x 12 = 142.15
1/02-7/02	(330x59.71%)/7 x 12 = 337.78	(183x59.71%)/7 x 12 = 187.32	(147x59.71%)/7 x 12 = 150.46

	Restated Annual Financial <u>Statements</u>
2004	508
2003	395
2002	312(d)
2001	228
2000	159
1999	172

8/02-12/02	(d) $(312 \times 40.29\%)/5$
	$\times 12 = 301.68$
1/02-7/02	$(312 \times 59.71\%)/7$
	$\times 12 = 319.37$

APPENDIX E

SEC Reports on Administrative Procedures

SEC Reports on Administrative Procedures

	10/1/96-3/31/97	4/1/97-9/30/97
Matters Before the ALJ	45	41
Matters Before the Commission	9	6
Review of SRO Decisions	26	26
Interlocutory Motions	2	2
Stay Requests	10	16

	(a)	(b)
8/02-9/02	$(31 \times 30.47\%)/2$	$(10 \times 30.47\%)/2$
	$\times 6 = 28.34$	$\times 6 = 9.14$
4/02-7/02	$(31 \times 69.53\%)/4$	$(10 \times 69.53\%)/4$
	$\times 6 = 32.33$	$\times 6 = 10.43$

	10/1/97-3/30/98	4/1/98-9/30/98
Matters Before the ALJ	18	43
Matters Before the Commission	7	5
Review of SRO Decisions	18	16
Interlocutory Motions	0	0
Stay Requests	7	5

| 8/02-9/02 | (c)
(7x30.47%)/2

x 6 = 6.4 | (d)
(3x30.47%)/2

x 6 = 2.74 |
| 4/02-7/02 | (7x69.53%)/4

x 6 = 7.3 | (3x69.53%)/4

x 6 = 3.13 |

	10/1/98-3/31/99	4/1/99-9/30/99
Matters Before the ALJ	21	57
Matters Before the Commission	3	10
Review of SRO Decisions	11	22
Interlocutory Motions	1	1
Stay Requests	8	6

(e) (3x30.47%)/2
x 6 = 2.74
(3x69.53%)/4
x 6 = 3.13

	10/1/99-3/31/00	4/1/00-9/30/00
Matters Before the ALJ	10	31
Matters Before the Commission	9	6
Review of SRO Decisions	12	13
Interlocutory Motions	1	0
Stay Requests	4	13

	10/1/00-3/31/01	4/1/01-9/30/01
Matters Before the ALJ	10	27
Matters Before the Commission	8	5
Review of SRO Decisions	13	10
Interlocutory Motions	0	0
Stay Requests	5	3

	10/1/01-3/31/02	4/1/02-9/30/02
Matters Before the ALJ	19	31(a)
Matters Before the Commission	11	10(b)
Review of SRO Decisions	4	7(c)
Interlocutory Motions	2	3(d)
Stay Requests	7	3(e)

	10/1/02-3/31/03	4/1/03-9/30/03
Matters Before the ALJ	34	40
Matters Before the Commission	4	4
Review of SRO Decisions	11	10
Interlocutory Motions	0	0
Stay Requests	13	11

	10/1/03-3/31/04	4/1/04-9/30/04
Matters Before the ALJ	32	71
Matters Before the Commission	7	5
Review of SRO Decisions	15	13
Interlocutory Motions	1	0
Stay Requests	6	4

	10/1/04-3/31/05
Matters Before the ALJ	47
Matters Before the Commission	11
Review of SRO Decisions	12
Interlocutory Motions	0
Stay Requests	7

APPENDIX F

Unpaired T Test Printouts

Unpaired T Test Printouts

SEC Enforcement Statistice – FederalCourt Actions

WINKS 4.80a BASIC Edition   January 7, 2006

  Independent Group Analysis   C:\WINKS480\FEDCT.DBF

  Group Means and Standard Deviations

  1: mean = 39.0   s.d. = 11.5968   n = 34
  2: mean = 45.6829   s.d. = 9.8627   n = 41

  Mean Difference = -6.68293   Pooled s.d. = 2.51554

  Test for Equality of Variance

  This preliminary test determines which version of the t-test to perform.

  Test equality of variance: F = 1.38 with (33, 40) D.F. p = 0.327 (two-tail)

  Note: Since the p-value for equality of variance is greater than 0.05,
  use the Equal variance t-test results.

  Independent Group t-test Hypotheses

  Ho: There is no difference between means.
  Ha: The means are different.

  Independent Group t-test on Summary Data

    Equal variance: Calculated t= -2.7 with 73 D.F. p = 0.009 (two-tail)

  Unequal variance: Calculated t= -2.66 with 65.1 D.F. p = 0.01 (two-tail)

  (For a one-sided test, you must adjust the p-value according to
  the direction of your alternative hypothesis.)

  Confidence Interval

A 95% Confidence Interval about the mean difference is: (-11.6965 to -1.6694)

Based on a standard error of 2.5155 and a 0.05% t-statistic of 1.993 with 73 d.f.

SEC Enforcement Statistics - Admininstrative Law Judges Initial Decisions & Orders

WINKS 4.80a BASIC Edition   January 7, 2006

Independent Group Analysis   C:\WINKS480\INITIAL.DBF

Group Means and Standard Deviations

1: mean = 1.7059   s.d. = 1.1423   n = 34
2: mean = 2.5366   s.d. = 1.7044   n = 41

Mean Difference = -.8307   Pooled s.d. = .3305

Test for Equality of Variance

This preliminary test determines which version of the t-test to perform.

Test equality of variance: $F = 2.23$ with (40, 33) D.F. $p = 0.02$ (two-tail)
Note: Since the p-value for equality of variance is low, (less than 0.05)
use the Unequal variance t-test results.

Independent Group t-test Hypotheses

Ho: There is no difference between means.
Ha: The means are different.

Independent Group t-test on Summary Data

  Equal variance: Calculated $t= -2.42$ with 73 D.F. $p = 0.018$ (two-tail)

Unequal variance: Calculated $t= -2.51$ with 70.1 D.F. $p = 0.014$ (two-tail)

(For a one-sided test, you must adjust the p-value according to
the direction of your alternative hypothesis.)

Confidence Interval

A 95% Confidence Interval about the mean difference is: (-1.4894 to -0.172)

Based on a standard error of 0.3305 and a 0.05% t-statistic of 1.993 with 73 d.f.

SEC Enforcement Statistics - Administrative Proceedings

WINKS 4.80a BASIC Edition   January 7, 2006

Independent Group Analysis   C:\WINKS480\ADMIN.DBF

Group Means and Standard Deviations

1: mean = 28.0588   s.d. = 12.9777   n = 34
2: mean = 41.2927   s.d. = 13.3046   n = 41
Mean Difference = -13.23386   Pooled s.d. = 3.04482

Test for Equality of Variance

This preliminary test determines which version of the t-test to perform.

Test equality of variance: $F = 1.05$ with (40, 33) D.F. $p = 0.89$ (two-tail)

Note: Since the p-value for equality of variance is greater than 0.05,
use the Equal variance t-test results.

Independent Group t-test Hypotheses

Ho: There is no difference between means.
Ha: The means are different.

Independent Group t-test on Summary Data

  Equal variance: Calculated t= -4.34 with 73 D.F. $p <= 0.001$ (two-tail)

Unequal variance: Calculated t= -4.35 with 71.1 D.F. $p <= 0.001$ (two-tail)

(For a one-sided test, you must adjust the p-value according to
the direction of your alternative hypothesis.)

Confidence Interval

185

A 95% Confidence Interval about the mean difference is: (-19.3023 to -7.1654)

Based on a standard error of 3.0448 and a 0.05% t-statistic of 1.993 with 73 d.f.

SEC Enforcement Statistics – Commission Opinions

WINKS 4.80a BASIC Edition   January 7, 2006

Independent Group Analysis   C:\WINKS480\COMMO.DBF

Group Means and Standard Deviations

1: mean = 2.1471   s.d. = 1.6901   n = 34
2: mean = 3.9756   s.d. = 2.815   n = 41

Mean Difference = -1.82855   Pooled s.d. = .52659

Test for Equality of Variance

This preliminary test determines which version of the t-test to perform.

Test equality of variance: $F = 2.77$ with (40, 33) D.F. $p = 0.003$ (two-tail)

Note: Since the p-value for equality of variance is low, (less than 0.05)
use the Unequal variance t-test results.

Independent Group t-test Hypotheses

Ho: There is no difference between means.
Ha: The means are different.

Independent Group t-test on Summary Data

  Equal variance: Calculated t= -3.32 with 73 D.F. $p \le 0.001$ (two-tail)

Unequal variance: Calculated t= -3.47 with 67 D.F. $p \le 0.001$ (two-tail)

(For a one-sided test, you must adjust the p-value according to
the direction of your alternative hypothesis.)

Confidence Interval

A 95% Confidence Interval about the mean difference is: (-2.8781 to -0.779)

Based on a standard error of 0.5266 and a 0.05% t-statistic of 1.993 with 73 d.f.

SEC Enforcement Statistics – Trading Suspensions

WINKS 4.80a BASIC Edition   January 7, 2006

Independent Group Analysis   C:\WINKS480\TRADESU.DBF

Group Means and Standard Deviations

1: mean = .7059   s.d. = 1.0009   n = 34
2: mean = 1.3902   s.d. = 1.6413   n = 41

Mean Difference = -.68436   Pooled s.d. = .30849

Test for Equality of Variance

This preliminary test determines which version of the t-test to perform.

Test equality of variance: $F = 2.69$ with (40, 33) D.F. $p = 0.004$ (two-tail)

Note: Since the p-value for equality of variance is low, (less than 0.05)
use the Unequal variance t-test results.

Independent Group t-test Hypotheses

Ho: There is no difference between means.
Ha: The means are different.

Independent Group t-test on Summary Data

  Equal variance: Calculated t= -2.12 with 73 D.F. $p = 0.037$ (two-tail)

Unequal variance: Calculated t= -2.22 with 67.5. D.F. $p = 0.03$ (two-tail)

(For a one-sided test, you must adjust the p-value according to
the direction of your alternative hypothesis.)

Confidence Interval

A 95% Confidence Interval about the mean difference is: (-1.2992 to -0.0695)

Based on a standard error of 0.3085 and a 0.05% t-statistic of 1.993 with 73 d.f.

CFTF Reports – Total SEC Enforcement Actions Filed

WINKS 4.80a BASIC Edition   June 1, 2005

Independent Group Analysis   C:\WINKS480\SECTOTAL.DBF

Group Means and Standard Deviations

1: mean = 529.84   s.d. = 63.6556   n = 3
2: mean = 586.1733   s.d. = 87.9851   n = 3

Mean Difference = -56.33333   Pooled s.d. = 62.69877

Test for Equality of Variance

This preliminary test determines which version of the t-test to perform.

Test equality of variance: F = 1.91 with (2, 2) D.F. p = 0.687 (two-tail)

Note: Since the p-value for equality of variance is greater than 0.05,
use the Equal variance t-test results.

Independent Group t-test Hypotheses

Ho: There is no difference between means.
Ha: The means are different.

Independent Group t-test on Summary Data

  Equal variance: Calculated t= -.9 with 4 D.F.   p = 0.42 (two-tail)

Unequal variance: Calculated t= -.9 with 3.6 D.F.   p = 0.425 (two-tail)

(For a one-sided test, you must adjust the p-value according to
the direction of your alternative hypothesis.)

Confidence Interval

A 95% Confidence Interval about the mean difference is: (-230.4468 to 117.7802)

Based on a standard error of 62.6988 and a 0.05% t-statistic of 2.777 with 4 d.f.

CFTF Reports – Financial Fraud and Issuer Reporting Actions Filed

WINKS 4.80a BASIC Edition   June 1, 2005

Independent Group Analysis   C:\WINKS480\FINFRAUD.DBF

Group Means and Standard Deviations

1: mean = 126.4267   s.d. = 33.0894   n = 3
2: mean = 154.6533   s.d. = 45.5438   n = 3

Mean Difference = -28.22667   Pooled s.d. = 32.50203

Test for Equality of Variance

This preliminary test determines which version of the t-test to perform.

Test equality of variance: $F = 1.89$ with (2, 2) D.F. $p = 0.691$ (two-tail)

Note: Since the p-value for equality of variance is greater than 0.05,
use the Equal variance t-test results.

Independent Group t-test Hypotheses

Ho: There is no difference between means.
Ha: The means are different.

Independent Group t-test on Summary Data

  Equal variance: Calculated t= -.87 with 4 D.F. $p = 0.434$ (two-tail)

Unequal variance: Calculated t= -.87 with 3.7 D.F. $p = 0.439$ (two-tail)

(For a one-sided test, you must adjust the p-value according to
the direction of your alternative hypothesis.)

Confidence Interval

A 95% Confidence Interval about the mean difference is: (-118.4843 to 62.031)

Based on a standard error of 32.502 and a 0.05% t-statistic of 2.777 with 4 d.f.

CFTF Reports – Officer and Director Bars Sought

WINKS 4.80a BASIC Edition   June 1, 2005

Independent Group Analysis   C:\WINKS480\O&D.DBF

Group Means and Standard Deviations

1: mean = 78.6533   s.d. = 41.981   n = 3
2: mean = 147.44   s.d. = 24.5345   n = 3

Mean Difference = -68.78667   Pooled s.d. = 28.07336

Test for Equality of Variance

This preliminary test determines which version of the t-test to perform.

Test equality of variance: F = 2.93 with (2, 2) D.F. p = 0.509 (two-tail)

Note: Since the p-value for equality of variance is greater than 0.05,
use the Equal variance t-test results.

Independent Group t-test Hypotheses

Ho: There is no difference between means.
Ha: The means are different.

Independent Group t-test on Summary Data

  Equal variance: Calculated t= -2.45 with 4 D.F. p = 0.07 (two-tail)

Unequal variance: Calculated t= -2.45 with 3.2 D.F. p = 0.087 (two-tail)

(For a one-sided test, you must adjust the p-value according to
the direction of your alternative hypothesis.)

Confidence Interval

A 95% Confidence Interval about the mean difference is: (-146.746 to 9.1726)

Based on a standard error of 28.0734 and a 0.05% t-statistic of 2.777 with 4 d.f.

CFTF Reports – Temporary Restraining Orders Filed

WINKS 4.80a BASIC Edition   June 1, 2005

Independent Group Analysis   C:\WINKS480\TEMPREST.DBF

Group Means and Standard Deviations

1: mean = 37.4533   s.d. = 9.4982   n = 3
2: mean = 39.0667   s.d. = 6.1978   n = 3

Mean Difference = -1.61333   Pooled s.d. = 6.54802

Test for Equality of Variance

This preliminary test determines which version of the t-test to perform.

Test equality of variance: F = 2.35 with (2, 2) D.F. p = 0.597 (two-tail)

Note: Since the p-value for equality of variance is greater than 0.05,
use the Equal variance t-test results.

Independent Group t-test Hypotheses

Ho: There is no difference between means.
Ha: The means are different.

Independent Group t-test on Summary Data

  Equal variance: Calculated t= -.25 with 4 D.F. p = 0.818 (two-tail)

Unequal variance: Calculated t= -.25 with 3.4 D.F.   p = 0.82 (two-tail)

(For a one-sided test, you must adjust the p-value according to
the direction of your alternative hypothesis.)

Confidence Interval

A 95% Confidence Interval about the mean difference is: (-19.7971 to 16.5704)

Based on a standard error of 6.548 and a 0.05% t-statistic of 2.777 with 4 d.f.

CFTF Reports – Asset Freezes

WINKS 4.80a BASIC Edition   June 1, 2005

Independent Group Analysis   C:\WINKS480\FREEZES.DBF

Group Means and Standard Deviations

1: mean = 54.16   s.d. = 10.3632   n = 3
2: mean = 49.24   s.d. = 10.913   n = 3

Mean Difference = 4.92   Pooled s.d. = 8.68887

Test for Equality of Variance

This preliminary test determines which version of the t-test to perform.

Test equality of variance: $F = 1.11$ with (2, 2) D.F. $p = 0.948$ (two-tail)

Note: Since the p-value for equality of variance is greater than 0.05,
use the Equal variance t-test results.

Independent Group t-test Hypotheses

Ho: There is no difference between means.
Ha: The means are different.

Independent Group t-test on Summary Data

 Equal variance: Calculated t= .57 with 4 D.F. $p = 0.601$ (two-tail)

Unequal variance: Calculated t= .57 with 4. D.F. $p = 0.602$ (two-tail)

(For a one-sided test, you must adjust the p-value according to
the direction of your alternative hypothesis.)

Confidence Interval

A 95% Confidence Interval about the mean difference is: (-19.2089 to 29.0489)

Based on a standard error of 8.6889 and a 0.05% t-statistic of 2.777 with 4 d.f.

CFTF Reports – Subpoena Enforcement Proceedings

WINKS 4.80a BASIC Edition   June 1, 2005

 Independent Group Analysis   C:\WINKS480\SUBPOENA.DBF

 Group Means and Standard Deviations

 1: mean = 14.0467   s.d. = 5.6309   n = 3
 2: mean = 13.0933   s.d. = 4.7356   n = 3

 Mean Difference = .95333   Pooled s.d. = 4.24785

 Test for Equality of Variance

This preliminary test determines which version of the t-test to perform.

Test equality of variance: $F = 1.41$ with (2, 2) D.F. $p = 0.829$ (two-tail)

Note: Since the p-value for equality of variance is greater than 0.05,
use the Equal variance t-test results.

Independent Group t-test Hypotheses

Ho: There is no difference between means.
Ha: The means are different.

Independent Group t-test on Summary Data

  Equal variance: Calculated t= .22 with 4 D.F. $p = 0.833$ (two-tail)

Unequal variance: Calculated t= .22 with 3.9 D.F. $p = 0.834$ (two-tail)

(For a one-sided test, you must adjust the p-value according to
the direction of your alternative hypothesis.)

Confidence Interval

A 95% Confidence Interval about the mean difference is: (-10.8429 to 12.7495)

Based on a standard error of 4.2478 and a 0.05% t-statistic of 2.777 with 4 d.f.

Financial Statement Restatements – Restatements by Year Filed

WINKS 4.80a BASIC Edition   August 24, 2005

  Independent Group Analysis   C:\WINKS480\RESTMTS.DBF

Group Means and Standard Deviations

1: mean = 264.195   s.d. = 53.9887   n = 4
2: mean = 352.0333   s.d. = 53.7001   n = 3

Mean Difference = -87.83833   Pooled s.d. = 41.10875

Test for Equality of Variance

This preliminary test determines which version of the t-test to perform.

Test equality of variance: F = 1.01 with (3, 2) D.F. p = 0.935 (two-tail)

Note: Since the p-value for equality of variance is greater than 0.05,
use the Equal variance t-test results.

Independent Group t-test Hypotheses

Ho: There is no difference between means.
Ha: The means are different.

Independent Group t-test on Summary Data

  Equal variance: Calculated t= -2.13 with 5 D.F. p = 0.086 (two-tail)

Unequal variance: Calculated t= -2.14 with 4.5 D.F. p = 0.093 (two-tail)

(For a one-sided test, you must adjust the p-value according to
the direction of your alternative hypothesis.)

Confidence Interval

A 95% Confidence Interval about the mean difference is: (-193.5289 to 17.8522)

Based on a standard error of 41.1087 and a 0.05% t-statistic of 2.571 with 5 d.f.

Financial Statement Restatements – Audited 10K Restatements by Year Filed

WINKS 4.80a BASIC Edition   August 24, 2005

Independent Group Analysis   C:\WINKS480\10K.DBF

Group Means and Standard Deviations

1: mean = 135.33   s.d. = 38.6952   n = 4
2: mean = 212.0   s.d. = 38.3536   n = 3

Mean Difference = -76.67   Pooled s.d. = 29.40514

Test for Equality of Variance

This preliminary test determines which version of the t-test to perform.

Test equality of variance: F = 1.02 with (3, 2) D.F. p = 0.939 (two-tail)

Note: Since the p-value for equality of variance is greater than 0.05,
use the Equal variance t-test results.

Independent Group t-test Hypotheses

Ho: There is no difference between means.
Ha: The means are different.

Independent Group t-test on Summary Data

  Equal variance: Calculated t= -2.6 with 5 D.F. p = 0.048 (two-tail)

Unequal variance: Calculated t= -2.61 with 4.5 D.F. p = 0.054 (two-tail)

(For a one-sided test, you must adjust the p-value according to
the direction of your alternative hypothesis.)

Confidence Interval

A 95% Confidence Interval about the mean difference is: (-152.2706 to -1.0694)

Based on a standard error of 29.4051 and a 0.05% t-statistic of 2.571 with 5 d.f.

Financial Statement Restatements – Audited 10Q Restatements by Year Filed

WINKS 4.80a BASIC Edition   August 24, 2005

Independent Group Analysis   C:\WINKS480\10Q.DBF

Group Means and Standard Deviations

1: mean = 128.87   s.d. = 21.1291   n = 4
2: mean = 140.0667   s.d. = 22.0774   n = 3

Mean Difference = -11.19667   Pooled s.d. = 16.5554

Test for Equality of Variance

This preliminary test determines which version of the t-test to perform.

Test equality of variance: F = 1.09 with (2, 3) D.F. p = 0.881 (two-tail)

Note: Since the p-value for equality of variance is greater than 0.05,
use the Equal variance t-test results.

Independent Group t-test Hypotheses

Ho: There is no difference between means.
Ha: The means are different.

Independent Group t-test on Summary Data

  Equal variance: Calculated t= -.68 with 5 D.F. p = 0.526 (two-tail)

Unequal variance: Calculated t= -.68 with 4.3 D.F. p = 0.534 (two-tail)

(For a one-sided test, you must adjust the p-value according to
the direction of your alternative hypothesis.)

Confidence Interval

A 95% Confidence Interval about the mean difference is: (-53.7606 to 31.3673)

Based on a standard error of 16.5554 and a 0.05% t-statistic of 2.571 with 5 d.f.

Financial Statement Restatements – Restated Annual Financial Statements

WINKS 4.80a BASIC Edition   August 24, 2005
```
-----------------------------------------------------------------------
```
Independent Group Analysis   C:\WINKS480\RESTATED.DBF
```
-----------------------------------------------------------------------
```
Group Means and Standard Deviations
```
----------------------------------
```
1: mean = 219.5925   s.d. = 72.9446   n = 4
2: mean = 401.56   s.d. = 103.3163   n = 3

Mean Difference = -181.9675   Pooled s.d. = 69.91648

Test for Equality of Variance
```
-----------------------------
```

This preliminary test determines which version of the t-test to perform.

Test equality of variance: F = 2.01 with (2, 3) D.F. p = 0.56 (two-tail)

Note: Since the p-value for equality of variance is greater than 0.05,
use the Equal variance t-test results.

Independent Group t-test Hypotheses
```
------------------------------------
```

Ho: There is no difference between means.
Ha: The means are different.

Independent Group t-test on Summary Data
```
-----------------------------------------------------------------------
```
  Equal variance: Calculated t= -2.76 with 5 D.F. p = 0.04 (two-tail)

Unequal variance: Calculated t= -2.6 with 3.5 D.F.   p = 0.071 (two-tail)

(For a one-sided test, you must adjust the p-value according to
the direction of your alternative hypothesis.)

Confidence Interval
```
-------------------
```

A 95% Confidence Interval about the mean difference is: (-361.7227 to -2.2123)

Based on a standard error of 69.9165 and a 0.05% t-statistic of 2.571 with 5 d.f.

SEC Reports on Administrative Proceedings – Matters Before the Administrative Law Judges

WINKS 4.80a BASIC Edition   August 24, 2005

Independent Group Analysis   C:\WINKS480\ALJM.DBF

Group Means and Standard Deviations

1: mean = 29.5275   s.d. = 14.7794   n = 12
2: mean = 42.0567   s.d. = 15.6242   n = 6

Mean Difference = -12.52917   Pooled s.d. = 7.67389

Test for Equality of Variance

This preliminary test determines which version of the t-test to perform.

Test equality of variance: $F = 1.12$ with (5, 11) D.F. $p = 0.811$ (two-tail)

Note: Since the p-value for equality of variance is greater than 0.05, use the Equal variance t-test results.

Independent Group t-test Hypotheses

Ho: There is no difference between means.
Ha: The means are different.

Independent Group t-test on Summary Data

  Equal variance: Calculated t= -1.67 with 16 D.F. $p = 0.115$ (two-tail)

Unequal variance: Calculated t= -1.63 with 9.6 D.F. $p = 0.135$ (two-tail)

(For a one-sided test, you must adjust the p-value according to the direction of your alternative hypothesis.)

Confidence Interval

A 95% Confidence Interval about the mean difference is: (-28.798 to 3.7397)

Based on a standard error of 7.6739 and a 0.05% t-statistic of 2.12 with 16 d.f.

SEC Reports on Administrative Proceedings – Matters Before the Commission

WINKS 4.80a BASIC Edition   August 24,2005

Independent Group Analysis   C:\WINKS480\COMM.DBF

Group Means and Standard Deviations

1: mean = 7.4525   s.d. = 2.5101   n = 12
2: mean = 6.69   s.d. = 2.8984   n = 6

Mean Difference = .7625   Pooled s.d. = 1.3875

Test for Equality of Variance

This preliminary test determines which version of the t-test to perform.

Test equality of variance: $F = 1.33$ with (5, 11) D.F. $p = 0.64$ (two-tail)

Note: Since the p-value for equality of variance is greater than 0.05,
use the Equal variance t-test results.

Independent Group t-test Hypotheses

Ho: There is no difference between means.
Ha: The means are different.

Independent Group t-test on Summary Data

  Equal variance: Calculated $t = .58$ with 16 D.F. $p = 0.571$ (two-tail)

Unequal variance: Calculated $t = .55$ with 8.9 D.F. $p = 0.596$ (two-tail)

(For a one-sided test, you must adjust the p-value according to
the direction of your alternative hypothesis.)

Confidence Interval

A 95% Confidence Interval about the mean difference is: (-2.179 to 3.704)

Based on a standard error of 1.3875 and a 0.05% t-statistic of 2.12 with 16 d.f.

SEC Reports on Administrative Proceedings – Review of Self-Regulatory Organization Decisions

WINKS 4.80a BASIC Edition   August 24, 2005

Independent Group Analysis   C:\WINKS480\SRO.DBF

Group Means and Standard Deviations

1: mean = 14.8583   s.d. = 7.0003   n = 12
2: mean = 11.2333   s.d. = 2.9269   n = 6

Mean Difference = 3.625   Pooled s.d. = 2.34765

Test for Equality of Variance

This preliminary test determines which version of the t-test to perform.

Test equality of variance: F = 5.72 with (11, 5) D.F. p = 0.067 (two-tail)

Note: Since the p-value for equality of variance is greater than 0.05,
use the Equal variance t-test results.

Independent Group t-test Hypotheses

Ho: There is no difference between means.
Ha: The means are different.

Independent Group t-test on Summary Data

  Equal variance: Calculated t= 1.2 with 16 D.F. p = 0.247 (two-tail)

Unequal variance: Calculated t= 1.54 with 15.8 D.F. p = 0.142 (two-tail)

(For a one-sided test, you must adjust the p-value according to

the direction of your alternative hypothesis.)

Confidence Interval

A 95% Confidence Interval about the mean difference is: (-1.3521 to 8.6021)

Based on a standard error of 2.3477 and a 0.05% t-statistic of 2.12 with 16 d.f.

SEC Reports on Administrative Proceedings – Interlocutory Motions

WINKS 4.80a BASIC Edition   August 24, 2005

Independent Group Analysis   C:\WINKS480\INTERLOC.DBF

Group Means and Standard Deviations

1: mean = 1.0108   s.d. = 1.0675   n = 12
2: mean = .6233   s.d. = 1.1114   n = 6

Mean Difference = .3875   Pooled s.d. = .54849

Test for Equality of Variance

This preliminary test determines which version of the t-test to perform.

Test equality of variance: $F = 1.08$ with (5, 11) D.F. $p = 0.842$ (two-tail)

Note: Since the p-value for equality of variance is greater than 0.05,
use the Equal variance t-test results.

Independent Group t-test Hypotheses

Ho: There is no difference between means.
Ha: The means are different.

Independent Group t-test on Summary Data

  Equal variance: Calculated t= .72 with 16 D.F. $p = 0.484$ (two-tail)

Unequal variance: Calculated t= .71 with 9.7 D.F. $p = 0.496$ (two-tail)
(For a one-sided test, you must adjust the p-value according to

the direction of your alternative hypothesis.)

Confidence Interval

A 95% Confidence Interval about the mean difference is: (-0.7753 to 1.5503)

Based on a standard error of 0.5485 and a 0.05% t-statistic of 2.12 with 16 d.f.

SEC Reports on Administrative Proceedings – Stay Requests

WINKS 4.80a BASIC Edition   August 24, 2005

Independent Group Analysis   C:\WINKS480\STAY.DBF

Group Means and Standard Deviations

1: mean = 7.2608   s.d. = 3.9904   n = 12
2: mean = 7.29   s.d. = 3.9911   n = 6

Mean Difference = -.02917   Pooled s.d. = 1.99543

Test for Equality of Variance

This preliminary test determines which version of the t-test to perform.

Test equality of variance: $F = 1.0$ with (5, 11) D.F. $p = 0.922$ (two-tail)

Note: Since the p-value for equality of variance is greater than 0.05,
use the Equal variance t-test results.

Independent Group t-test Hypotheses

Ho: There is no difference between means.
Ha: The means are different.

Independent Group t-test on Summary Data

  Equal variance: Calculated t= -.01 with 16 D.F. $p = 0.989$ (two-tail)

Unequal variance: Calculated t= -.01 with 10.1 D.F. $p = 0.989$ (two-tail)

(For a one-sided test, you must adjust the p-value according to

202

the direction of your alternative hypothesis.)

Confidence Interval

A 95% Confidence Interval about the mean difference is: (-4.2595 to 4.2012)

Based on a standard error of 1.9954 and a 0.05% t-statistic of 2.12 with 16 d.f.

APPENDIX G

Chi Square Printouts

Chi Square Printouts

Web Chi Square Calculator: Results

	Column 1	Column 2	Column 3	Column 4	Column 5	Column 6	Column 7	Column 8	Total
				Federal Court Actions					
Post-SOX	164	144	192	157	174	160	211	196	1398
Pre-SOX	198	198	168	134	135	173	142	126	1274
Total	362	342	360	291	309	333	353	322	2672

Degrees of freedom: 7
Chi-square = 43.6114682167915
p is less than or equal to 0.001.
The distribution is significant.

	Column 1	Column 2	Column 3	Column 4	Column 5	Column 6	Column 7	Column 8	Total
			Administrative Law Judges Initial Decisions and Orders						
Post-SOX	10	13	18	14	6	9	9	8	87
Pre-SOX	8	6	9	4	6	6	8	9	56
Total	18	19	27	18	12	15	17	17	143

Degrees of freedom: 7
Chi-square = 5.61811562092068
For significance at the .05 level, chi-square should be greater than or equal to 14.07.
The distribution is not significant.
p is less than or equal to 1.

	Column 1	Column 2	Column 3	Column 4	Column 5	Column 6	Column 7	Column 8	Total
				Administrative Proceedings					
Post-SOX	176	163	193	219	200	122	150	164	1387
Pre-SOX	130	119	113	121	108	131	107	75	904
Total	289	282	306	340	308	253	257	239	2274

Degrees of freedom: 7
Chi-square = 29.3803777631069
p is less than or equal to 0.001.
The distribution is significant.

	Commission Opinions								
	Column 1	Column 2	Column 3	Column 4	Column 5	Column 6	Column 7	Column 8	Total
Post-SOX	13	11	12	21	14	12	25	26	134
Pre-SOX	12	8	8	10	11	12	3	5	69
Total	25	19	20	31	25	24	28	31	203

Degrees of freedom: 7
Chi-square = 18.1349270753342
p is less than or equal to 0.025.
The distribution is significant.

Total SEC Enforcement Actions Filed				
	Column 1	Column 2	Column 3	Total
Post-SOX	504	679	575.5	1758.5
Pre-SOX	602.5	484	503	1589.5
Total	1106.5	1163	1078.5	3348

Degrees of freedom: 2
Chi-square = 37.903510031798
p is less than or equal to 0.001.
The distribution is significant.

Financial Fraud and Issuer Reporting Actions Filed				
	Column 1	Column 2	Column 3	Total
Post-SOX	108	199	156.9	463.9
Pre-SOX	164.2	112	103	379.2
Total	272.2	311	259.9	843.1

Degrees of freedom: 2
Chi-square = 39.0036573282889
p is less than or equal to 0.001.
The distribution is significant.

Officer and Director Bars Sought			
	Column 1	**Column 2**	**Column 3**	**Total**
Post-SOX	151	170	121.2	442.2
Pre-SOX	126.9	51	58	235.9
Total	277.9	221	179.2	678.1

Degrees of freedom: 2
Chi-square = 28.3136994917452
p is less than or equal to 0.001.
The distribution is significant.

Temporary Restraining Orders Filed			
	Column 1	**Column 2**	**Column 3**	**Total**
Post-SOX	36	35	46.2	117.2
Pre-SOX	48.36	31	33	112.36
Total	84.36	66	79.2	229.56

Degrees of freedom: 2
Chi-square = 4.1531493863511
For significance at the .05 level, chi-square should be greater than or equal to 5.99.
The distribution is not significant.
p is less than or equal to 0.20.

Asset Freezes			
	Column 1	**Column 2**	**Column 3**	**Total**
Post-SOX	48	39	60.66	147.66
Pre-SOX	63.47	43	56	162.47
Total	111.47	82	116.66	310.13

Degrees of freedom: 2
Chi-square = 1.8251426862977
For significance at the .05 level, chi-square should be greater than or equal to 5.99.
The distribution is not significant.
p is less than or equal to 1.

Subpoena Enforcement Proceedings

	Column 1	Column 2	Column 3	Total
Post-SOX	9	12	18.3	39.3
Pre-SOX	19.14	15	8	42.14
Total	28.14	27	26.3	81.44

Degrees of freedom: 2
Chi-square = 7.93164107243183
p is less than or equal to 0.025.
The distribution is significant.

Restatements by Year Filed

	Column 1	Column 2	Column 3	Total
Post-SOX	414	323	319.1	1056.1
Pre-SOX	337.7	270	233	840.7
Total	751.7	593	552.1	1896.8

Degrees of freedom: 2
Chi-square = 1.46708966310391
For significance at the .05 level, chi-square should be greater than or equal to 5.99.
The distribution is not significant.
p is less than or equal to 1.

Audited 10K Restatements by Year Filed

	Column 1	Column 2	Column 3	Total
Post-SOX	253	206	176.9	635.9
Pre-SOX	187.3	140	98	425.3
Total	440.3	346	274.9	1061.2

Degrees of freedom: 2
Chi-square = 3.37694136570563
For significance at the .05 level, chi-square should be greater than or equal to 5.99.
The distribution is not significant.
p is less than or equal to 0.20.

Audited 10Q Restatements by Year Filed

	Column 1	Column 2	Column 3	Total
Post-SOX	161	117	142.1	420.1
Pre-SOX	150.4	130	135	415.4
Total	311.4	247	277.1	835.5

Degrees of freedom: 2
Chi-square = 1.20055123791807
For significance at the .05 level, chi-square should be greater than or equal to 5.99.
The distribution is not significant.
p is less than or equal to 1.

Restated Annual Financial Statements

	Column 1	Column 2	Column 3	Total
Post-SOX	508	395	301.6	1204.6
Pre-SOX	319.3	228	159	706.3
Total	827.3	623	460.6	1910.9

Degrees of freedom: 2
Chi-square = 2.1616128555928
For significance at the .05 level, chi-square should be greater than or equal to 5.99.
The distribution is not significant.
p is less than or equal to 1.

Matters Before the Administrative Law Judges

	Column 1	Column 2	Column 3	Column 4	Column 5	Column 6	Total
Post-SOX	47	71	32	40	34	28.34	252.34
Pre-SOX	32.33	19	27	10	31	10	129.33
Total	79.33	90	59	50	65	38.34	381.67

Degrees of freedom: 5
Chi-square = 22.8171285724138
p is less than or equal to 0.001.
The distribution is significant.

Matters Before the Commission

	Column 1	Column 2	Column 3	Column 4	Column 5	Column 6	Total
Post-SOX	11	5	7	4	4	9.14	40.14
Pre-SOX	10.43	11	5	8	6	9	49.43
Total	21.43	16	12	12	10	18.14	89.57

Degrees of freedom: 5
Chi-square = 3.40600984886167
For significance at the .05 level, chi-square should be greater than or equal to 11.07.
The distribution is not significant.
p is less than or equal to 1.

Review of Self-Regulatory Organization Decisions

	Column 1	Column 2	Column 3	Column 4	Column 5	Column 6	Total
Post-SOX	12	13	6.4	11	10	15	67.4
Pre-SOX	7.3	4	10	13	13	12	59.3
Total	19.3	17	16.4	24	23	27	126.7

Degrees of freedom: 5
Chi-square = 7.10200300659745
For significance at the .05 level, chi-square should be greater than or equal to 11.07.
The distribution is not significant.
p is less than or equal to 1.

Stay Requests

	Column 1	Column 2	Column 3	Column 4	Column 5	Column 6	Total
Post-SOX	7	4	6	11	13	2.74	43.74
Pre-SOX	3.13	7	3	5	13	4	35.13
Total	10.13	11	9	16	26	6.74	78.87

Degrees of freedom: 5
Chi-square = 4.9006764114878
For significance at the .05 level, chi-square should be greater than or equal to 11.07.
The distribution is not significant.
p is less than or equal to 1.

APPENDIX H

Survey

D. De Vay Doctoral Dissertation
"The Effectiveness of the Sarbanes-Oxley Act of 2002 on the Prevention and Detection of Fraud in Financial Statements"

Your Name :
Firm's Name:
Your Position in the Firm:
Please mark or highlight your responses.

1. Sarbanes-Oxley has changed the way accountants perform audits
   - Strongly Agree
   - Agree
   - No Opinion
   - Disagree
   - Strongly Disagree
2. Sarbanes-Oxley has changed the way companies perform their accounting tasks.
   - Strongly Agree
   - Agree
   - No Opinion
   - Disagree
   - Strongly Disagree
3. The attitude of company management toward the audit has changed due to Sarbanes-Oxley.
   - Strongly Agree
   - Agree
   - No Opinion
   - Disagree
   - Strongly Disagree
4. There are more work-related opportunities for accountants because of Sarbanes-Oxley.
   - Strongly Agree
   - Agree
   - No Opinion
   - Disagree
   - Strongly Disagree
5. The benefits of Sarbanes-Oxley are worth the cost.
   - Strongly Agree
   - Agree
   - No Opinion
   - Disagree
   - Strongly Disagree
6. Sarbanes-Oxley is effective in the prevention and detection of fraud in financial statements.
   - Strongly Agree

- o Agree
- o No Opinion
- o Disagree
- o Strongly Disagree

7. Sarbanes-Oxley should be modified.
   - o Strongly Agree
   - o Agree
   - o No Opinion
   - o Disagree
   - o Strongly Disagree

8. Sarbanes-Oxley should be eliminated.
   - o Strongly Agree
   - o Agree
   - o No Opinion
   - o Disagree
   - o Strongly Disagree

Comments:

May I use your name and your firm's name in my dissertation?
- o Yes
- o No

APPENDIX I

Survey Responses

Survey Responses

Question #	CPAs	CFOs & CAOs	COOs	CEOs	VP	Other	Total Executives	All Totals
1								
Strongly Agree	4	23	1	2	5	5	36	40
Agree	2	5	1		1	1	8	10
No Opinion							0	0
Disagree	1						0	1
Strongly Disagree	1						0	1
2								
Strongly Agree	3	16	1	2	1	1	21	24
Agree	3	9	1		3	5	18	21
No Opinion							0	0
Disagree	1	3			2		5	6
Strongly Disagree	1						0	1
3								
Strongly Agree		4	1	1	1	1	8	8
Agree		8			2	2	12	12
No Opinion							0	0
Disagree					1	1	2	2
Strongly Disagree							0	0
4								
Strongly Agree	5	21	1	2	6	4	34	39
Agree	3	7	1			2	10	13
No Opinion							0	0
Disagree							0	0
Strongly Disagree							0	0
5								
Strongly Agree	1	1			1		2	3
Agree	1	2					2	3
No Opinion	1	3				1	4	5

	NASDAQ	NYSE	AMEX	OTC	Pink Sheets	Private	Totals	
Disagree	2	13	2	1	3	3	22	24
Strongly Disagree	3	9		1	2	2	14	17
6								
Strongly Agree		1			1		2	2
Agree	3	7	1	1	3	1	13	16
No Opinion	3	5				1	6	9
Disagree	1	12	1	1	1	2	17	18
Strongly Disagree	1	3			1	2	6	7
7								
Strongly Agree	3	19	2	2	2	3	28	31
Agree	1	9			3	2	14	15
No Opinion	3					1	1	4
Disagree	1				1		1	2
Strongly Disagree							0	0
8								
Strongly Agree	1	1		1			2	3
Agree	3	5		1		1	7	10
No Opinion						1	1	1
Disagree	3	19	2		4	2	27	30
Strongly Disagree	1	3			2	2	7	8
Totals	56	208	15	15	46	46	330	386

	Company Executives						
	Public					Private	
Question #	NASDAQ	NYSE	AMEX	OTC	Pink Sheets		Totals
1							
Strongly Agree	13	8	2	1	1	11	36
Agree	3	1				4	8
No Opinion							0
Disagree							0
Strongly Disagree							0

2

	C1	C2	C3	C4	C5	C6	Total
Strongly Agree	5	4	1			11	21
Agree	9	4	1	1		3	18
No Opinion							0
Disagree	2	1			1	1	5
Strongly Disagree							0

3

	C1	C2	C3	C4	C5	C6	Total
Strongly Agree	3	3		1		1	8
Agree	6	2	1			3	12
No Opinion							0
Disagree	2						2
Strongly Disagree							0

4

	C1	C2	C3	C4	C5	C6	Total
Strongly Agree	13	7	2		1	11	34
Agree	3	2		1		4	10
No Opinion							0
Disagree							0
Strongly Disagree							0

5

	C1	C2	C3	C4	C5	C6	Total
Strongly Agree						2	2
Agree	2						2
No Opinion	1	1				2	4
Disagree	7	6				9	22
Strongly Disagree	6	2	2	1	1	2	14

6

	C1	C2	C3	C4	C5	C6	Total
Strongly Agree	1					1	2
Agree	6	4				3	13
No Opinion	3		1			2	6
Disagree	5	3		1		8	17
Strongly Disagree	1	2	1		1	1	6

7

Strongly Agree	11	5	2	1	1	8	28
Agree	5	4				5	14
No Opinion						1	1
Disagree						1	1
Strongly Disagree							0

8

Strongly Agree		1	1				2
Agree	3		1		1	2	7
No Opinion	1						1
Disagree	10	6		1		10	27
Strongly Disagree	2	2				3	7
Totals	123	68	15	8	7	109	330

Comments "This is possibly the biggest and worst modification of securities law since it was enacted." (CFO-Public, Pink Sheets)
"What we need is to eliminate SEC reviews of micro cap companies and ease restrictions on legended stock." (CFO-Public, Pink Sheets)
"We are a private company so the cost and full implications have not hit us." (CFO-Private)
"Small practitioners were not the problem. Big 4 are the problem. They control the AICPA and make all the rules to benefit themselves then they violate the rules and we are expected to clean up their problems." (CPA, Partner-CPA Firm)
"Accountants that do what they should have all along - don't make problems." (CPA, Partner-CPA Firm)
"We do not do any 'public work.' But, it is a good idea to have the accountants do the extra fraud work. It also makes the management of companies accountable, which is necessary for public companies. Our audit standards have changed as a direct result of SO. I think the effect of SO is overkill for the smaller organizations and may not be as cost effective as with the public companies." (CPA, Partner-CPA Firm)
Sarbanes-Oxley should be eliminated "if not changed." (CPA, Managing Member-CPA Firm)
"Sarbanes-Oxley does very little that auditors should not have already been doing. The larger auditing firms seem to have disregarded what they already were required to do. For non-public firms, all

Sarbanes-Oxley accomplished was to add cost with little or no benefits." (CPA, Managing Member-CPA Firm)

SOX administration is difficult, for smaller companies and CPAs. Section 404 requires more documentation. It is costing $4-10 million dollar companies to spend hundreds of thousands of dollars, and expect it to continue for 4-5 years. SOX is unnecessary in total. The SEC should make executives sign off on the financials and then have stronger measures for punishment. There was good planning for SOX, and it was not passed too quickly. It is just unnecessary. The AICPA was doing just fine before SOX. (CPA, Managing Partner-CPA Firm)

"In my opinion, S/O is knee jerk reaction to very preventable fraud. Congress wanted to pass something to appear to be doing something. If not for Enron, the fraud referred to here has gone on since the beginning of business history." (Principal-Private)

"Sarbanes-Oxley has mainly affected public companies. Private companies like [respondent company] have been affected only to a small degree." (CFO-Private)

On if the benefits of SOX are worth the cost. "Jury is out we will not know for a number of years." (CFO-Private)

On whether SOX is effective in prevention and detection of fraud in financial statements. "We do not know the impact my guess is some impact not sure enough to be considered an effective prevention." (CFO-Private)

"[SOX] should be modified but I wouldn't eliminate it entirely!" (VP Controller-Public, NASDAQ)

"Overall, SOX has resulted in a significant amount of additional work, much higher audit fees and a reduction of operational effectiveness for us with minimal benefit." (VP Controller-Public, NASDAQ)

"SOX was needed, but the legislation was too hasty and went farther than was/is wise. It has and will help companies become more disciplined and thoughtful about controls and having management teams take more care in filing and disclosing results. Mike Oxley, who I know and I believe is a very good and serious congressman, and his staff, did not fully realize how much power they were inadvertently investing in the (now) less competitive accounting profession. Very concerning how much time US registered senior execs are spending on this admittedly important area of controls, at the expense of not spending time and focus on becoming more competitive and nimble, at the very moment that competition is becoming more global, more tough, and so many foreign registered companies do not have the same level of regulatory oversight and resource requirements. SOX was a good thing but, overall, does not yet have the balance that solid legislation should, I believe, reflect." (CFO-Public, NYSE)

"Monopolistic power of auditors. Companies pay 2 or 3 times more, especially w/PCAOB dues. Consultants charge more than high priced auditors. Companies have to pay for the learning curve. Congress can set a tone, but cannot always adhere to the regulations. Should Congress legislate ethics? Senior executives spend too much time on SOX to the detriment of the corporation. Foreign companies do not have to deal with SOX. Competitiveness problem. Sarbanes will survive, but it should be modified and I hope it is modified." (CFO-Public, NYSE)

"I believe that SOX could be effective to prevent fraudulent financial reporting and create an effective and efficient control environment if top management encourage and supports full compliance and they do not override key controls in place." (CPA, Managing Director-CPA Firm)

"Sarbanes-Oxley will not prevent accounting irregularities. The tone set at the top of an organization is the most important control. If executive management does not set the proper tone of expecting compliance with all laws and regulations, employees will continue to act as they have in the past." (CFO-Public, NASDAQ)

"Fraud was always illegal. While tightening BOD requirements, etc., is beneficial, additional documentation of processes that firms do not ordinarily keep is a tremendous waste." (CFO-Private)

"You need to separate Sarbox in general, which I believe overall is very positive, from Section 404 of Sarbox which is definitely NOT worth the effort." (CFO-Public, NASDAQ)

"SOX should be revised to reduce the cost and workload to a more reasonable standard." (CFO-Public, NASDAQ)

"Sarbanes Oxley Act has increased Executive Management awareness and involvement in Internal Controls over Financial Reporting. However, the current certification process, which is highly influenced by ASB2, has a low ROI for the companies and may not provide adequate focus on Fraud prevention and detection." (VP, Corporate Audit-Public, NASDAQ)

"Cost of complying with SOX requirements far exceed the benefits for small centralized companies, particularly in the real estate arena. This excludes the intangible of management time involved in the process." (SVP-Finance-Public, NYSE)

"For [respondent company] this [SOX] was really an internal control documentation and testing exercise. [Attitude of company management toward audit changed due to SOX] depends on level of management. Not worth year 1 costs; hopefully this process becomes more efficient. It [SOX] certainly helps but is not a guarantee ALL fraud will be detected or prevented." (CPA, SVP - Finance and Accounting/Treasurer- Public, NASDAQ)

"The principles of SOX are well intended but industry and the regulators need to reach a workable balance between cost and benefit specifically as we consider global competitiveness of the US economy. No system can be designed to detect and prevent all fraud but systems and vigilance can make it harder to perpetrate." (Chief Audit & Risk Officer-Public, NYSE)

"Though compliance with SOX has been very onerous for companies, it has achieved much of what it was intended to achieve. Companies are definitely dedicating more time and attention to accounting and financial reporting which has resulted in higher quality financial statements." (Director of SOX Compliance-Public, NYSE)

"Management focus and subsequent findings has improved business unit awareness and knowledge related to the [Company's] significant processes and controls and their responsibilities within the overall control environment. While we believe that this outcome is laudable we have strong reservations related to the costs of the overall effort relative to the benefits potentially gained. We suggest the following for review:

1. Evaluate the need for tiers of risk that would allow companies to perform testing on a periodic basis as opposed to annually...
2. Allow open and free dialogue between management and external auditors...
3. Greater clarity related to the interpretation of the standards must be provided."

(Vice President-Public, NYSE)

"Sarbox has definitely had an impact on industry. Most important, it has caused revaluations of certain companies due to required restatements, once problems were found." (CFO, Private)

Printed in the United Kingdom
by Lightning Source UK Ltd.
119627UK00001BA/11